Praise for *You'll* ⌐

"What a fun book, brimming wit⌐ ⌐ ⌐ insights from screenwriter Jean Shepherd, and written with humor and wisdom." —**Sue Stewart, author of *My Christmas Story Story* (special edition, 2023)**

"*Don't Shoot Your Eye Out!* is one of those rare reads that will make you laugh and leave you all the wiser for it. Schultze reveals why *A Christmas Story* is a timeless movie classic. With humorous personal insights from author Jean Shepherd and engaging life lessons from the movie, Schultze reminds us 'to dream our way forward in life.' Skip your therapy session this week, and read this wonderful celebration of life. You won't regret it. —**David McFadzean, co-creator of the TV show *Home Improvement***

"Dr. Schultze explains how Jean Shepherd told stories, and even provides a straightforward, seven-step guide for writers, teachers, and public speakers. Highly recommended for the Shep fan in all of us!" —**Mark Adams, publisher of "The Jean Shepherd Show" YouTube Channel**

"A thoughtful and entertaining look at the stories behind *A Christmas Story*! Discover why the movie truly resonates with so many of us, year after year." —**Brian Jones, founder, The House from A Christmas Story, in Cleveland, Ohio**

"Hey, that nasty little toady Grover Dill from *A Christmas Story* called a timeout from bullying kids just to read this intriguing book. He said the amazing life lessons in *A Christmas Story* might save him from an eventual life behind bars. What a great read, filled with homegrown humor and plenty of wisdom!" —**Yano Anaya (aka Grover Dill in the movie), Co-owner of https://www.achristmasstoryfamily.com/**

"Schultze's book brilliantly peels back the layers of *A Christmas Story*, and reveals with humor and delight the process of Jean Shepherd's masterful storytelling. Buy copies for your friends and family who love the movie—it will be far better than an ugly tie, a blue bowling ball, or even pink bunny pajamas!" —**Nick Mantis, creator of the forthcoming video documentary, "*Shep*"—*The Life & Career of Master Storyteller Jean Shepherd***

"Quentin Schultze brilliantly uncovers and illustrates *A Christmas Story*'s life lessons, showing how popular culture conveys practical and even spiritual truths." —**Mark Pinsky, author of *The Gospel According to the Simpsons* and *The Gospel According to Disney***

"This book is a great read *and* loaded with practical, down-to-earth wisdom—a rare combination today."—**Coleman Luck, Hollywood writer/executive producer known for the *The Equalizer* television series (1985–1989)**

"*You'll Shoot Your Eye Out!* is a terrific book that takes us behind the scenes of the holiday classic. Amazing!"—**Craig Detweiler, Dean of the College of Arts & Media, Grand Canyon University, and author of *Honest Creativity: The Foundations of Boundless, Good, and Inspired Innovation***

"My family and I love watching *A Christmas Story*. Thanks to Dr. Schultze's great book, we will now enjoy the movie even more." —**Mike Huckabee, former Governor, Arkansas**

"Schultze's friendship with Jean Shepherd and his amazing knowledge of the stories behind the script make this a must-read book for all fans." —**Dave Svoboda, "Kid with Goggles" in *A Christmas Story***

"Even as a 40-year fan of *A Christmas Story*, I learned many new, fascinating, and fun things about the film, the screenwriter, and the 'secret' life lessons in the movie. This amazing book should win a major award." —**John Demmer, co-author of the forthcoming book, *The Extras of* A Christmas Story: *Amazing Film Trivia from the Unknown "Stars" of the Movie***

Purchase signed copies of the book, dedicated personally to your friends and family, using the QR Code, above, or this address online: https://quentin-schultze.square.site/

# YOU'LL SHOOT YOUR EYE OUT!

# YOU'LL SHOOT YOUR EYE OUT!

### Life Lessons from the Movie
### A *Christmas Story*

Dr. Quentin Schultze

*edenridge press* LLC

Published by
Edenridge Press LLC
Grand Rapids, Michigan USA
service@edenridgepress.com
Quantity discounts and personally signed copies available at:
quentin-schultze.square.site

Edited by Robert Banning, Turning Leaves Editorial.
Cover design and interior line drawings by Richard Trebus.
Interior design and typesetting by PerfecType, Nashville, TN.
Ebook design by Steven Chevalia.
Proofed by Elizabeth Banks.

Schultze, Quentin
Title: You'll shoot your eye out! life lessons from the movie a Christmas story /
Quentin Schultze

Library of Congress Control Number: 2024939811

ISBN 978-1-937532-01-7 (alk. Paper)

PER004030
PERFORMING ARTS / Film / History & Criticism

HUM020000
HUMOR / Topic / Celebrity & Popular Culture

Subjects: LCSH: Christmas story (Motion picture). | Christmas films—United
States—History and criticism. | Shepherd, Jean.

# Acknowledgments

**M**any kind souls have encouraged me and offered solid editorial advice, including Steve Glazer, Dave Hartwell, Mark Fackler, John Demmer, Joel Baumwoll, and Chad Allen.

I also gained special insights about the movie, *A Christmas Story*, and screenwriter Jean Shepherd, from Nick Mantis and Sue Stewart—along with Glazer.

Professionals who helped in the editing, design, proofing, and digital conversion of this book include Bob Banning, Kristin Goble, Elizabeth Banks, and Steven Chevalia (see the copyright page). Rich Trebus deserves special recognition for his outstanding cover and line-drawing designs.

My indefatigable literary agent, Chris Ferebee, is a gem.

When I was a wet-behind-the-ears, rambunctious professor at Calvin College in Michigan during the early 1980s, my department chair and teaching colleague, Professor Dave Holquist, encouraged me to contact Jean Shepherd and provided amazing support. Dave even made a noose-around-the-neck tie to use in class with Jean (Shepherd fans will recall the tinfoil-noose story from the book *In God We Trust: All Others Pay Cash*). Without Dave, this book would not exist. I miss him, a real mensch.

# Contents

# CONTENTS

# Introduction

Everyone cheers for Ralphie, the dreamy kid in *A Christmas Story* who wants a Red Ryder 200-shot range model air rifle for Christmas. And we all boo Scut Farkus, the bully with yellow eyes who harasses Ralphie and his buddies. We laugh at Ralphie's Old Man, who wins the risqué leg lamp and places it triumphantly in the front window to "turn on" his Cleveland Street neighbors.

And we all know the repeated warning to Ralphie, "You'll shoot your eye out!"

But there are deeper messages in the movie. *A Christmas Story* humorously conveys life lessons on topics such as pursuing dreams, being flexible, distrusting the media, playing fair, and being an everyday hero—like Mom.

I knew Jean Shepherd, the film's screenwriter, who died in 1999. We cotaught a university course about his storytelling, including the vignettes in *A Christmas Story*. Through our collaboration and friendship, I learned how he used humorous stories to capture his "secret" lessons about life.

I wrote this book from the insights I gained while teaching and conversing with Shepherd. I kept elaborate notes for instructing my university students about how his stories function as "parables" (stories about everyday life meant to capture deeper life lessons). In this book, I reveal those insights in print for the first time.

Shepherd was especially attuned to how children see the marvelous but confusing world around them. He realized that there is a lot of childlike wonder in adults too. The character Ralphie represents each one of us, regardless of our age.

The overall film is a tale about dreaming our way forward in life, with marvel and delight, in a bewildering world. How bewildering? Even Santa and his elves are unpleasant! We dare each other to be foolish—like putting our tongues on a frozen flagpole. The media cajole us into believing silly things that we want to believe anyway. We struggle with verbal if not physical bullies. And so much more. Life can be fun, but it's not always easy. Just ask Ralphie!

As I illuminate the life lessons in *A Christmas Story*, you'll enjoy the film even more. And you won't have to lock yourself in the bathroom, like Ralphie, to secretly decipher my messages with your Ovaltine decoder ring. I decipher the movie messages for you. Best of all, there is no "crummy commercial" in this book, although I hope you like the book so well that you will give copies to your friends and family. After all, they might need a lift in life—even to the top of Santa's thirty-foot mountain at your local department store.

After reading this book, you can impress your friends and family with your movie genius: "Do you think Mom broke the leg lamp accidentally or on purpose? Why? What was wrong with the major award—or with its winner, the Old Man, who earned it with Mom's help in the first place?" What's the life lesson here? I'll share with you what the screenwriter told me.

Before we delve into the movie's life lessons, I would like to address some common misconceptions about the film and screenwriter Shepherd's humor.

*First,* A Christmas Story *is not merely nostalgia.* Shepherd and his gifted director, Bob Clark, aimed for a timeless movie. They used the approximate year of 1940 in order to set the scene for an ageless classic, not just to re-create family, school, and neighborhood life in the upper Midwest during that period. The nostalgia is entertaining, but the film's life lessons are timeless. In my view, the enduring life lessons are what make the movie so rewatchable; the stories ring "true" with our experiences, generation after generation.

*Second, the movie is not primarily autobiographical.* Shepherd borrowed many names and remembrances from his childhood in Hammond, Indiana. Some of the character names are taken from actual people in his life, especially his childhood friends and neighbors. A "Miss Shields" was Shepherd's second-grade teacher during the 1928 Christmas season. As I explain in the book, however, he also developed ideas from the media and from other people's life experiences. He told me that he was creating a character who ran "Qwazy Quentin's Car Lot"; his idea was that professors (like me) are akin to used-car salespersons, peddling recycled ideas instead of cars. Ouch!

*Third, the adult Ralphie is not merely a narrator.* The older and wiser Ralphie is a character in the movie. In this book, I use the name "Shep" (short for "Shepherd") to refer to the mature Ralphie. Screenwriter Shepherd, playing the voice of the adult Ralphie, injects himself into the stories to give us clues about the movie's life lessons. He's not a third-party, detached narrator, such as we hear in documentary films.

*Fourth,* A Christmas Story *is primarily uplifting humor.* The movie aims to be compassionate toward most of its characters, most of the time. Shepherd disliked comedy that is self-righteously critical of others. In his view, too much comedy is created to make fun of people or to shock audiences with crude language.

Shepherd's style of *humor* (from the same root word as "humility") helps us to identify humbly with the characters. His humor leads us to laugh *at ourselves*. In *A Christmas Story*, we are invited to identify with the characters through their victories and travails—and thereby to discover *with* them what they are learning about life in a good-but-imperfect world.

I wrote this book using the kind of humorous, character-loving storytelling that Shepherd taught me. I entertain you while helping you "decode" Shepherd's marvelous stories. I use humorous illustrations from my own life to show how Shepherd's lessons apply to today's family situations and to grandparenting as well as parenting.

Because *A Christmas Story* is so popular with kids who might want to read this book, I decided to hide some of the letters in the obscene and profane language that I quote from the movie and the shooting script. I serve parents whose early-reading kids love the movie and want to read the book. Every adult reader will know which words I am referring to anyway (just like we all know what Ralphie uttered instead of "fudge").

One overarching theme in Shepherd's many stories is that even the ordinary, simple things in life are important. We should humbly (with humor) treasure life together, one day at a time. If we can't laugh at ourselves along the way, we are in trouble; the Bumpus hounds or the furnace clinkers will drive us nutty.

Thanks very much for journeying with me as I decode Shepherd's life lessons from *A Christmas Story*. Just be careful along the way. Humor can ricochet. You might discover that Shepherd is talking about you, you rascal! Eat your "beetloaf" gratefully and, if necessary, break your old man's leg-lamp obsession before he makes a neighborhood fool of himself. Along the way, don't shoot your eye out. Ho, ho, ho!

# CHAPTER 1

# Pursue Your Dreams

In an early scene in *A Christmas Story*, Ralphie, his buddies, and his little brother, Randy, are staring nose-to-glass in the display window at Higbee's department store. We see their faces from the point of view of the toys in the window. Shep says, "First-nighters, packed earmuff to earmuff, jostled in wonderment before a gold, tinkling display of mechanized, electronic joy."

The window-shopping kids are dreaming. Imagining. What do they really, truly want for Christmas? What are their hearts' desires?

Ralphie has eyes for only one item, which Shep calls the "holy grail of Christmas gifts. The Red Ryder 200-shot range model air rifle." What a beauty!

Ralphie looks longingly at the cardboard display image of Red Ryder, seemingly larger than life, one of the most popular Western heroes of the day. The cowboy star is cradling Ralphie's dream gift. Shep says it was "Red Ryder himself. In his hand was the knurled stock of as coolly, deadly looking a piece of weaponry as ever I had laid eyes on."

Then we witness Ralphie through the glass again, mouthing Red Ryder's own words on the promotional poster copy for the rifle: "It's all yours, Little Beaver. . . . This 200-shot range model air rifle is just like the one I used in my range wars chasin' rustlers and bad guys." Little Beaver was the name of Red Ryder's trusty young Navajo companion.

Ralphie had already been smitten for weeks. The gun was his simmering, night-and-day dream. Hardly anything else mattered. Ralphie absolutely had to get his hands on the knurled stock of one of those rifles so he could chase the bad guys that were undoubtedly roaming around Cleveland Street, looking for victims like the Parker family. Evil was real. So were heroes. Comic books and radio shows made that abundantly clear to Ralphie as he pondered his next move to acquire the weapon.

Ralphie's real-life dream for the rifle is so strong that it captures his daydreaming. When he submits his class theme on what he wants for Christmas, he and his teacher, Miss Shields, are suddenly transported into a kind of Victorian romance. She dons a feathered hat. Her heart is fluttering. She wondrously gives Ralphie an A+ grade on his paper, and then continues adding pluses on the blackboard, like love letters to her brilliant pupil. Tchaikovsky's love theme from his *Romeo and Juliet* plays in the background.

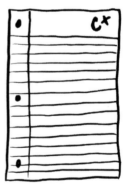

Through that wild scene, we're all invited to witness the imaginary literary romance between a sterling student and a raptured fourth-grade teacher. We can feel Ralphie's glory through the images and especially the music. We are with him on his wistful adventure. Ralphie might be dreamily naïve, but we love him! Go for it, Ralphie. Make your dream come true. Miss Shields loves you for your literary genius!

## Why Does the Movie Use Dream Scenes?

Ralphie dreams about shooting the bad guys in the backyard, getting an A+ on his theme paper, and returning home as an adult to show his parents that he has gone blind from sucking on soap. Such dream scenes are designed to help us experience Ralphie's own feelings more deeply. Shepherd called it "expressionism"— distorting *external* reality (what we see and hear) to better capture Ralphie's *internal* reality (what he actually feels).

Adolescents and adults also experience heart-grabbing dreams. I recall wanting a car when I turned sixteen. Actually, I didn't just *want* one; I felt like I *had* to have one. My personal freedom and public image were at stake. As Shepherd told me, young men and cars are romantic partners; many guys even give their cars female names.

Our human dreams are never satisfied. As soon as I was able to buy an old Volkswagen (VW) Beetle by working two jobs, I fantasized about owning a better vehicle. I was just puttering around town in my rackety little air-cooled bug while some of my friends were zooming down the streets in monster V8s that could lay rubber. I felt like Little Beaver—not Red Ryder. I kept dreaming.

Today, I dream about being the world's best grandfather. Ironically, I never even knew my paternal grandfather, who abandoned the family. He was a womanizer, renowned in vaudeville as "The Amazing Karl with the One-String Cigar-Box Fiddle." Not exactly a role model, although I admire his entrepreneurial spirit and clever branding. I imagine winning the love of my grandchildren—and I nurture their love partly by giving them the toys of *their* dreams.

The Old Man in the movie dreamed about winning a major award. He diligently answered brain-numbing questions in newspaper puzzles and submitted his answers in hopes of hitting it big. He aimed to prove to others and himself that he had astonishing "mind power." Clearly, he was not particularly talented at the contests. Mom had to clue him in on the historic name of the Lone Ranger's nephew's horse: Victor. The puzzle was called "Name the Great Characters of American Literature." Was the literary giant the nephew or the stallion?

Shepherd told me that one important life lesson in *A Christmas Story* is to pursue our dreams, without worrying about what others will think. He said that those who never dream about the future tend to get stuck in the past, often becoming mired in resentments. They cease imagining a better life and act accordingly.

Shepherd told me that those who truly dream are life's winners. I think there is something to that, both in *A Christmas Story* and in the real world. We all need to dream, even to dream big sometimes. No dreams, no hope. No hope, no motivation. We might as well sit in front of the television all day or surf social media. Shepherd also said that when a loser discovers someone who has more talent than they do, the loser is more likely to become resentful than to improve their lot in life.

When a dream goes sour, we just need to begin dreaming again. Ralphie keeps his dream alive even as the odds decrease that he will get the rifle for Christmas, especially after Santa pushes him down the slide. Ho, ho, ho! This is one of the most likable aspects of Ralphie; he keeps dreaming without getting angry or resentful, except, perhaps, when he pounds the daylights out of Farkus after receiving a mediocre grade on his what-I-want-for-Christmas theme paper.

Near the end of *A Christmas Story*, Ralphie has a run-in with a ricocheting BB. His earthly dream of getting the rifle seems to have turned into a minor tragedy, softened by Mom's comfort. But soon he's drifting off to sleep, dreaming yet again of using his wonderful gift. We humans dream day and night.

## Is Grover Dill Being Groomed for a Life of Crime?

One of the major dream-less characters in *A Christmas Story* is Grover Dill, the toady to chief bully Scut Farkus. What does he truly desire in life? To become like his mentor, Scut? Maybe. But for now, all Dill can look forward to is laughing at other kids and getting pounded on the shoulder by Scut. Farkus is a budding gang leader who thinks he can control the neighborhood—that's a real dream. Dill is just a loser underling. Farkus is the CEO while Dill doesn't even have a job title. Dill needs a much bigger life dream. Shepherd suggested to me it might be a job as a hit man for the mob, a seamless transition.

A guy in a massive Chevy station wagon ran into my poor little VW bug. My putterer was totaled; his monster had minor bumper damage. It was David versus Goliath when he clobbered me while he flew out of a K-Mart parking lot like a madman. I hired an attorney, added some of my savings to the insurance loot, and bought a speedy Chevelle. You never know! God seems to work in mysterious ways to make some of our dreams come true.

Shepherd and I both got into the hobby of amateur (ham) radio by listening to commercial AM radio stations across the eastern United States. Shepherd eventually hosted a nightly radio program on WOR in New York City—a powerhouse that covered most of the country east of the Mississippi. He told stories to thousands of listeners, young and old, capturing their imaginations. His nightly ratings were phenomenal; he attracted tens of thousands of young fans who still praise his storytelling. They dreamed of listening to his stories every night in bed, with their transistor radios hidden under their pillows.

Every year, Shepherd spun a version of the main tale in *A Christmas Story*, about Ralphie dreaming for the Red Ryder rifle and nearly shooting his eye out. Listeners loved it. The accolades of his fans were among Shepherd's dreams—just like writing the screenplay to *A Christmas Story* and seeing it on the big screen.

Bob Clark, who directed *A Christmas Story*, was smitten by Shepherd's storytelling when he first heard the radio raconteur's shows on a Florida station. Clark's immediate dream was to make a movie based on Shepherd's stories. It took Clark over twelve years, and his dream only came true because his film *Porky's* did so well financially. The studio wanted him to make a post-*Porky's* hit, but Clark held out for a deal that would enable him to make the lower-budget *A Christmas Story* as well, and even invested some of his own funds in the project. Quite an ironic story: *Porky's* debauchery funds a family flick.

*A Christmas Story* opened for Thanksgiving in 1983 and didn't do very well at the box office. It was pulled from most theaters before Christmas Day. But as VCRs and cable TV became popular, the movie unexpectedly took off and became a phenomenal hit. If Clark and Shepherd had lived to see their dream movie become so wildly popular, they would have been stunned as well as delighted. Their dream became true posthumously. In 2012, the movie was selected for preservation in the prestigious U.S. National Film Registry by the Library of Congress for being "culturally, historically or aesthetically significant."

If we have a dream, we likely have related passion. And with passion, often we are fascinated by something. The combination of passion and fascination will motivate us to grow our talents. Shepherd never lost his passion or his fascination for storytelling; he was always learning, trying new ways of entertaining people and being humorous. Fear keeps us from developing and using our talents.

## This Book Is My Dream Come True

Early in my university-teaching career, I contacted Shepherd to see if he would teach me storytelling. He was a master at it. He made my dream come true by teaching storytelling with me at a university. I was amazed at his insights and abilities. I think he responded to my request because he was flattered that a professor was taking his work seriously. Actually, I dreamt that one day I would author a book about his storytelling—using my own stories along with his tales. This is that book.

Shepherd was so fearless that he would try just about any of his new stories on nearly any audiences through any available medium. He loved storytelling. When he bombed, he learned. When he did extremely well, he amazed himself—at least early in his career.

In *A Christmas Story*, Shepherd offers the life lesson that pursuing even seemingly unachievable dreams is an important part of what it means to flourish in life. Of course, Ralphie dreamed of getting the BB rifle, day and night. It gave him a purpose—persuading others to make sure that he fulfilled his dream. I can imagine him becoming a great salesperson; he's learning the craft at a young age! The real Shepherd, as Ralphie, would have gotten back in line to pitch Santa with his gift wish a second time—without accepting any flak from the elves during the return trip.

Let's all pursue dreams, like Ralphie and the Old Man. Of course, we might make fools of ourselves along the way. Big deal! Let's set our sights on things that will give us deep pleasure and deliver joy to others.

And when our dreams turn sour?

Keep dreaming! Maybe even for a Red Ryder 200-shot range model air rifle. You won't hear me warn you about shooting your eye out. I've got a similar rifle I use to warn squirrels not to eat my bird seed. One shot in a squirrel's rear-end is usually enough to keep the varmint away for a few days. I dream of a squirrel-free feeder flooded with delightful chickadees, one BB at a time. So far, no ricochets.

## CHAPTER 2

# Curtail Your Obsessions

**S**hep describes Ralphie's drive for the Red Ryder BB rifle as a "mania." Desiring the rifle is not a bad thing, but what about Ralphie's unbridled drive to get one? Is he over the top?

Ralphie is so obsessed with acquiring the rifle that he even abandons a friend, Flick. When bullies Scut Farkus and Grover Dill descend upon Ralphie and his buddies in front of school, Ralphie takes off for the safety of the building. Shep says, "I left Flick to certain annihilation. But BB-gun mania knows no loyalties." Flick soon shuffles into the classroom with a black eye.

But Ralphie was desperate to win the support of his teacher, Miss Shields, for getting the rifle—as if she could make it happen. Some obsessions can make us irrational. As Jean Shepherd told me, our dreams can lead to fixations that make us daffy. He wasn't talking about obsessive-compulsive disorders. He was addressing the kind of unbridled passion that focuses our attention on just one dreamy goal, to the detriment of everything else in our lives.

One of the screenwriter's life lessons in *A Christmas Story* is that we need to curtail our dreams when they become extreme obsessions. Such out-of-control desires can even ruin our relationships with friends and family. We all know someone whose work or hobby has overshadowed all good sense; they seemingly will give up everything else to pursue that one thing. They are self-destroying devotees.

A sign that someone has gone too far is when their daydreams fuel their obsession. The problem is that we can't know about others' daydreams unless they tell us. We have to read their behaviors. Through the magic of the movie, Shepherd helps us experience Ralphie's daydreams.

How deep was Ralphie's dreamy obsession to be like Red Ryder? Early in the film, he imagines himself battling bad guys in the backyard, using his trusty rifle, dressed up like a cowpoke, spitting like a gunslinger.

## Why Did They Have to Stop Shooting the Black Bart Dream Scene?

They gave Peter Billingsley, who played Ralphie, real chewing tobacco for the cowboy dream scene where he proudly picks off the villains in his backyard. It made him quite sick. He recovered after a few hours, and filming proceeded. It's not easy being the spittin' image of a Western hero.

Ralphie daydreams about his family cowering under the kitchen table. "Save us, Ralphie," his quaking parents plead. Mom says, "I just knowed those bad guys would be coming for us in the end." The Old Man cries that the evil Black Bart is upon them. It's a scary situation. Ralphie must save the entire Parker clan. The baddies are hopping over the back fence, ready to invade the yard and then the house.

But no worries! Ralphie has Ol' Blue, the rifle. He peers down the barrel at the masked bandits. Best of all, Ralphie says, he's lucky that Ol' Blue has a compass in the stock. He will definitely need that in the gunfight! Who knows, Bart might attack from the north. Ralphie's dream is becoming a logic-killing obsession.

In Ralphie's daydream, the Old Man calls Ralphie a "deadeye" who is "getting them" bad guys. Bart and his gang better not return or they'll be "pushing up daisies," says Ralphie. Of course, Ol' Blue saves the day. The Old Man gives Ralphie the affirmation needed by a boy striving for manhood: "Well, son, you saved us." Salvation! Now that's something worth dreaming about!

## Why Doesn't the Old Man Ever Call Ralphie by Name?

Only in the blind-Ralphie dream scene does the Old Man call Ralphie by name, using the adult "Ralph." It's also the only time he refers to Ralphie as his own "son." In the car after the F-bomb incident, the Old Man whispers to Mom that Ralphie is "your son." Why? Shepherd believed that most fathers find it difficult to become emotionally connected with their sons; this was the case for Shepherd's actual father as well as for Shepherd's own relationship with his son.

Another obsession-demonstrating daydream scene with Ralphie was shot but not used. In that scene, Ralphie pretends to be the right-hand man for superhero Flash Gordon on the planet Mongo. Flash and Ralphie battle Ming the Merciless, who, according to Shep, "appears to be 18 feet tall, dressed in jade-green robes with sinister gold cabalistic symbols flashing in the unnatural light, his eyes glittering with an evil, Fu Manchu mustache adding to the horror, his yellow parchment skin ageless." Who wouldn't want to kill someone like that? He's a nightmare.

Planet Earth is in the balance during the battle between Ming and Flash. Suddenly, Ralphie enters the picture with his Red Ryder rifle. He shoots Ming dead. One shot. This time, it's Flash who affirms Ralphie's rifle obsession. Flash, his voice "quivering with reverent emotion," says, "It's the end of Ming the Merciless. You have done it Ralph [the adult name 'Ralph' is used in the shooting script for this scene]. You have saved all earthlings. You have saved our planet." Quite a feat for a young BB-gun hotshot. Once again, *salvation*—an ageless dream for all of us to prove ourselves by "saving" others in their times of need.

Ralphie was gripped with composing a persuasive theme paper for Miss Shields about what he wants for Christmas, the Red Ryder BB rifle. He thought he was creating a "magnificent, eloquent theme." And that such magnificence poured out of him naturally, with what Shep calls "feverish fluidity." He was on a dreamy rhetorical roll, imagining his teacher, Miss Shields, dubbing his theme "poetry," clearly the work of a "genius."

In Ralphie's daydream, Miss Shields gives him an A+ (with more pluses written on the blackboard), and flutters in delight. Reading his literary chef d'oeuvre, she experiences "ecstasy." Also, as a result, he imagines that "everyone" will suddenly "sympathize" with his heartfelt desire for the BB rifle. His persuasion will be perfectly executed because of his superb rhetorical prose. In earlier versions of the story, Ralphie dreamt that Miss Shields would visit the Parker home just to convince his parents that they needed to buy him the Red Ryder rifle for Christmas. She was so deeply moved by Ralphie's prose as to advocate for Ralphie getting a rifle.

So, what is Ralphie's great thematic work of rhetorical art? He fixatedly writes about "a Red Ryder BB gun with a compass in the stock . . . and this thing which tells time." "This thing" is truly masterful writing. Makes me flutter too.

Yet Ralphie convinces himself that he was being prepared his whole life to write the Red Ryder theme. He imagines that he was called to speak this earth-shattering truth, perhaps like Moses was called to persuade the Egyptians to let God's people go free. The problem is that Ralphie wasn't yet equipped. He had plenty of passion, but little ability. (Actually, Moses felt that way too and pleaded with God to send along his brother—the more eloquent Aaron.) It's painful to see Ralphie learn this life lesson. But we all do, sooner or later.

In real life, a dreamy obsession often runs ahead of talent. It makes it tougher to pursue our dreams successfully, partly because we don't want to do the necessary work to turn our dreams into reality. For Shepherd, too, one successful night on the radio or one laudable evening gig at The Limelight in New York City would not make him a great humorist. And it's more likely that we'll make even bigger fools of ourselves if we don't work toward our dreams. Few dreams come true as immediate miracles from on high.

One of the Old Man's dreams that became an obsession was winning a newspaper-puzzle contest. He works on the puzzles religiously, taking on even the most dreadfully difficult questions, like the name of the Lone Ranger's nephew's horse. The Old Man is determined to win one of the contests, to be admired by people near and far—or at least up and down the legendary Cleveland Street in Hohman, Indiana. He wants to win the prestigious but unspecified award, which would prove his great mind power. The Old Man prepares his pencils, sharpened and ready for action on the kitchen-table battlefield.

Bring on those obscure queries! The Old Man doesn't need erasers or a dictionary. All knowledge in heaven and on earth resides inside his oversize brain.

The Old Man was obsessed with these puzzles the way some addicts get hooked on daily crossword puzzles. My wife and I are vulnerable. We eventually decided to focus only on the Saturday crossword, doing it together. Otherwise, we might not accomplish anything else during the week. And we really go after each Saturday puzzle, making our dream come true by completing it almost every week—apart from a few stinker questions about the leading export of Bolivia or some young singer we never heard of.

The Old Man's sharp pencils and dull wit miraculously win the day (with Mom's help, of course, never acknowledged by the Old Man). The contest award is on the truck, heading to the Parker house. Home from work, the Old Man dances a jig in the living room. He tells Ralphie that winning such a prestigious award creates a real appetite (it's truly laborious work doing those puzzles, and the Old Man's noggin requires oodles of energy to function like a well-oiled Olds). Soon, the huge crate arrives and Ralphie retrieves a hammer and crowbar for his father to pry open the carton.

Mom must be glad that one of the questions on the newspaper puzzle was not about the origin of the word "fragile"; the Old Man slowly mispronounces it as "frah-JEE-lay," suggesting it's Italian. He tosses old-fashioned excelsior (puffy clutches of curled wood shavings that predated Styrofoam popcorn and other packing material) out of the crate like a dog scratching the grass, and holds up a leg in victory. Then comes the lamp shade, magnificently fringed, complementing the body tones in the faux leg. The Old Man's contest obsession has now been fulfilled in the form of a bizarre leg lamp. Or has it?

The Old Man's obsession only reaches its true maniacal zenith when he dashes outdoors in the dark of night to see the leg glowing perfectly, lusciously, in the exact center of the living room window. Shep says, "The entire neighborhood was turned on." Quite Freudian.

---

## Why Does the Leg-Lamp Shipping Crate Say "HIS END UP"?

The top of the shipping crate, which we see when it is being wheeled through the Parker door, says "HIS END UP" rather than "THIS END UP," because before shooting the scene the crew had to cut off part of the crate so it would fit through the door. The crate was made particularly large so the Old Man could get inside of it, fully immersing himself in the joy of unpacking his major award. For a few moments, the Old Man is an archeologist, digging through packing for his hidden treasure.

---

The lamp is so "glorious," so "indescribably beautiful," says Shep, that the Old Man loses the last vestiges of reason in his swelling brain. He tells Swede, the neighbor (played by the film's director, Bob Clark), that the shimmering leg is a "major award." Indeed, it is major—a major impending disaster for his marriage; spouses do not always share the same obsessions.

He can't see the leg lamp for what it really is, a tawdry piece of erotica. He can't just accept the lamp as a somewhat-less-than-major award and place it in a back room, away from all windows. He must broadcast his victory far and wide—"go tell it on the mountain," as the singers proclaim during the film's opening.

Mom breaks the lamp while alone in the living room, watering her plant. And she makes sure there is no glue in the house so the Old Man can't make a quick repair. Seething, the Old Man runs out for glue and soon tries to fix his turned-on passion in life. (I thought it would have been a great scene for the Olds not to start when he was heading to the store, requiring the Old Man to go to the Bumpuses, who offer him some "Victor" brand horse glue.)

---

## Why Did Mom Break the Leg Lamp?

Shepherd explained to me that Mom had to break the Old Man's fixation—not just the lamp. How could she live with a totally bonkers husband making a laughingstock of the Parker family and home? The newspaper puzzles were a private obsession—perfectly acceptable as long as he could also take care of other household duties, such as the clinking furnace and the dysfunctional Olds. But when an obsession goes public, everyone is in on it. It's like an alcoholic hitting the party scene and making a fool of himself by stumbling around and saying things he should later regret.

---

Finally, unable to reconstruct the lamp's broken plastic pieces, the Old Man mournfully buries the remains in the backyard. Shep says Ralphie might have heard a distant horn play taps to salute the fallen comrade, no longer so radiantly victorious. Dreams live and die. Obsessive ones die a bit harder—or more gloriously, depending on how you look at it.

Shepherd told me that the Old Man's obsessive "love" of the leg lamp reflects part of the human condition. We all tend to get infatuated with something—an activity, a piece of technology, a car, whatever. We just have to have it or do it. Even a wonderful dream becomes a stumbling block to sane living. And here's the scary part from Shepherd's angle on the lamp fiasco: Men get romantically involved with "things," especially technologies, to the point where they become irrational. In this sense, men are more romantic than women.

Sometimes we need others to curtail our overcooked, brain-frying obsessions. Mom saved the Old Man from his lunacy. She chuckles quietly in the background about it as he tries to repair the lamp in the front window.

And sometimes we feel like we must share our obsession with others, assuming that they will be impressed. Shepherd personally felt this way about classic cars. He stored one of his classic autos in the garage of his second wife and their two children—long after they were divorced and not exactly on speaking terms. The only time Shepherd ever went to that house was to get or return the car, not to visit his own ex or their children.

Shepherd was so smitten by cars that I couldn't drive anywhere with him where he didn't start commenting on the history and idiosyncrasies of vehicles and drivers. And he loved others' stories about their social, cultural, and financial entanglements with autos.

Sometimes our compulsive obsessions can settle down on their own and become dreamy enjoyments, without mania. For Ralphie, this will presumably happen with the Red Ryder rifle. His obsession starts to subside when a ricocheting BB hits him in the cheek. Shocked, he falls to the ground. Desperate to find his eyeglasses, he accidentally crushes them with his unbuckled galoshes. He will still love the rifle, but not quite so obsessively. He takes it to bed on Christmas night, falling into a real dream, during which he's "getting off spectacular hip shots" into the night. Some of our

deeper, more obsessive human dreams are fit only for nighttime fantasy, not daytime reality.

## Why Do Men Start Wars?

Shepherd said that men obsess far more than women. Men, he said, are incurably romantic toward gadgetry of all kinds, including weapons. Men start wars; they naturally feel like they have to use devices to gain power and control, to prove their manhood, to knock off the Black Barts and Mings of the world. They want to drive the hottest cars on the streets. And sometimes men will engage in such obsessive behavior even if they have to abandon their friends and embarrass their families along the way. In Shepherd's view, men just can't help themselves.

In *A Christmas Story*, Mom breaks the Old Man's lamp and, with it, his obsessive curse. Maybe he will still try to conquer the daily newspaper puzzles. So be it. He needs to dream. But when one of our dreams becomes a full-blown obsession, we probably need to be saved from it.

We all grow manic at times and want to put our lamp in the window to shout from the mountaintop that we have won the race before us. But when we get to the finish line, we wish that someone had stopped us along the way to curtail our nuttiness and help us enjoy life a bit more moderately, if not sanely. The best obsessions are frah-JEE-lay.

## CHAPTER 3

## Be Flexible

The Old Man helplessly watches as the Bumpus hounds invade the kitchen and haul off the delectably basted turkey on Christmas morning. He's left holding a wing. Great image! His dream of digging into a savory holiday feast just dashed out the door while he was reading the newspaper comics. He's caught in the real comedy of life.

Shep laments, "The heavenly aroma still hung heavy in the house. But it was gone. All gone. No turkey. No turkey sandwiches. No turkey salad. No turkey gravy, turkey hash, turkey a la king, or gallons of turkey soup. Gone. All gone!"

Shep masterfully sets up the Christmas-dinner catastrophe: "Sometimes, at the height of our revelries, when our joy is at its zenith, when all is most right with the world, the most unthinkable disasters descend upon us."

## Why Do the Parkers Prepare Turkey on Christmas?

The filmed turkey fiasco is based on Shepherd's written story about the Bumpus dogs stealing Mom's wonderfully baked ham on Easter. When the story was changed to Christmas, turkey seemed like a much more appropriate food, especially for the drama with the Bumpus hounds. By coincidence, the Chinese restaurant duck then seemed more like a direct visual replacement for the turkey—bird for bird.

We all dream. Sometimes we achieve our dreams. Other times, we get obsessive and have to curtail our dreams—or wait for someone else to curtail them for us.

At yet other times, we have to give up on our dreams. The painstakingly prepared turkey is gone forever. It has become feed for the stinkin' Bumpus hounds cohabitating under the porch next door. There will not be a turkey dinner this year at the Parker home. "All gone."

One of Jean Shepherd's lessons from *A Christmas Story* is that we have to learn to be flexible. Only fools think they can navigate smoothly through life's many surprises. Life throws unexpected curves at us—both challenges and opportunities. To put it simply, things happen. If we're not flexible, we become stagnant observers rather than active participants in the drama of daily existence.

A relative told me about arriving home from church on Thanksgiving Day to discover that the oven had died. The wonderfully prepared turkey was sitting in the oven, raw. No glorious turkey aroma. Just a cold, naked bird. Relatives were on the way, expecting a feast. What to do?

Using tin snips, she removed the turkey's backbone, put some butter under the skin, and flattened it out to cook on the backyard grill. Voilà! The bird roasted quickly. And it was delicious—even better than oven-baked birds, everyone agreed. People call it "spatchcocking" a bird. A potential disaster turned into a terrific meal—thanks to creative flexibility.

Shepherd told me that there are two basic ways to handle life's detours. One is to feel sorry for ourselves and likely give up. Those who do this are the *quitters*.

The other way is to briefly lick our wounds and start over again, on a new or perhaps a previously abandoned course. Those who respond this way are the *go-getters*, who make things happen in the world. Ironically, they often accomplish things that they themselves didn't even conceive. It's the creative art of changing gears in our thinking. Go-getters even turn around failure.

Shepherd believed that few of us have the stamina, courage, and especially the flexibility to be go-getters. We have difficulty changing course when things don't go our way. Why? First, we are too embarrassed to go back to a former way of doing things, thereby admitting we failed. We even feel shame. Second, we are afraid to try something new. We find safety and security in old ways of thinking and doing.

This is why Shepherd was always figuring out new ways of telling his stories for changing audiences. He never told the same story exactly the same way twice. He would even alter it during his telling, as he realized how a particular audience was responding. He saw the shifting audiences as new opportunities, not impossible difficulties. And he loved the immediacy of audience feedback more than he liked recording stories for the camera.

Shepherd's own life was fraught with struggles requiring flexibility. Once, he and his wife, Leigh Brown, were in Boston to work on a made-for-television production. The couple, great dog lovers, unthinkingly left their pooch in the car when they went to a meeting. The dog passed away in the heat. They were heartbroken. They didn't know if they could continue working on the production—ever. They just wanted to return home.

They decided instead to move forward in the midst of their mourning. They would personally dedicate their work on the show to the dog's memory. It was the same production that had brought them to Boston, but now with a revised motive. Sometimes flexibility comes from a change of heart.

One of the most revealing stories that Shepherd told me about his life fundamentally shaped my understanding of him and *A Christmas Story*. Shepherd said that his father came home from work one day and went to the couple's bedroom. Shepherd noticed that his dad was packing a suitcase. "What are ya' doin', Dad?" Shepherd asked. His father replied, "I'm leaving. You'll understand when you get older." Eventually his father remarried, but was never again part of Shepherd's life. I wonder, after that experience, how Shepherd could write a screenplay for a charming family movie such as *A Christmas Story*.

The answer seems to be that he was amazingly flexible, even emotionally. Down deep, he genuinely loved humankind, but he also hated parts of his own life and held many resentments toward others. He repeatedly disappointed himself and then acted like everything was fine. He would deal with his own failures and resentments by telling more humorous stories and gaining the appreciation of new audiences.

Shepherd learned the art of flexibility in his career. When he couldn't control the precise direction of his professional life, he would adapt to other opportunities. If there was a job in radio, he took it. TV opportunities? He accepted them. Stage and speaking? Short stories or novels? The same for all.

## Where Did the BB-Rifle Story First Appear?

Some of Shepherd's best-known stories, including the Red Ryder tale, were first published in *Playboy* magazine, of all places—twenty-three of them between 1964 and 1981. Why? Because Shepherd flexibly seized the opportunity to write for a magazine that, at the time, was trying to recruit gifted and even well-known literary authors. *Playboy* wanted to make itself a more legitimate magazine, and Shepherd wanted to prove that he could tell his oral tales in writing.

And here's the most amazing thing about Shepherd's flexibility—and why, as a communication teacher-scholar, I reached out to him in the first place: Shepherd taught himself how to adapt his bag of stories to any available medium. He told many of the vignettes from *A Christmas Story* on stage, on TV and video, in movies, over the radio, in his writings, and beyond. He could even perform his stories solo on the stage, acting out all of the major characters. Shepherd was a stunningly adaptable storyteller.

Shepherd had to be flexible because "the business"—as he liked to call entertainment—is mercurial. I wanted to learn storytelling, and he was the only person I could find in North America with a solid record of telling tales successfully across all available media. I discovered that he had become so adaptable out of necessity, being in show business. For his career, it was "be flexible or die."

In *A Christmas Story*, characters adjust to shifting situations. When Ralphie hears "You'll shoot your eye out" from one person, he moves on to the next one—all the way up to Santa Claus, whom Shep calls "the head honcho." Mom has to adapt to Randy's finicky eating, and especially to the Old Man's proclivities, from overloaded electrical circuits to battles with the furnace, and finally to the leg lamp itself. Ralphie has to be flexible in a world with bullies. Schwartz and Flick must adapt when the triple-dog-dare protocol is breached.

After Miss Shields gives Ralphie a demoralizing C+ grade on his grandiose theme about what he wants for Christmas, he's emotionally devastated. His dream of getting the rifle seems impossible. Walking home through the blighted yards, past the rusting carcass of an antique car, he passes a sign: "There is only one ORANGE CRUSH made from the whole fruit." Crushed, like poor Ralphie. He will have to try another approach—appealing to Santa, the man at the top of the mountain.

The Bumpus hounds get into the house to abscond with the turkey because Mom leaves the door unlatched when she retrieves the sobbing Ralphie from the backyard, after he's stung by the ricocheting BB. Smelling the scrumptious turkey on the table, the dogs easily break through the screen door, attack the golden fowl, and take off, leaving behind the lone wing that the Old Man holds up and briefly inspects—almost as if he might nonetheless devour it. That tiny turkey part wasn't sufficient for his ravenous appetite.

Instead of nibbling on the pathetic wing, the Old Man proclaims, "All right! Everybody upstairs. Get dressed. We are going out to eat." Indeed, they are, to the only restaurant open on Christmas Day—Bo Ling & Sons Chop Suey Palace. Afterward, Shep reports to viewers, "That Christmas would live in our memories as the Christmas when we were introduced to Chinese turkey." A fabulous memory. Very flexible, Old Man. And fun for the family. Much better than staying at home and chewing on cold meat loaf sandwiches made with soggy Wonder Bread.

## How Did They Make the Movie without Snow?

A big frustration during shooting the outdoor scenes in the winter of 1982 in Cleveland and in Canada was the lack of snow. The crew couldn't make adequate snow with the usual machines, even when the contraptions ran around the clock. They could truck in snow, but that was slow and expensive—and it melted quickly. Eventually, the film crew worked out a deal with the fire department to spray a white, foamy fire retardant that looked like snow and didn't quickly evaporate. But it was slippery. Actors and crew had to be careful. The movie could have become a slapstick comedy. For the falling snow in a few scenes, the crew used dehydrated potato flakes blown with fans.

I recall the time I cooked ribs on a tiny outdoor grill when my mother-in-law was visiting. We had just had our first child, and it was a wonderful day to celebrate together. I enjoy cooking and wanted to prepare the ribs perfectly. Well, I forgot they were on the grill. The ribs turned into hard lumps of charcoal, raw in the middle. They were so nasty looking and smelling that the Bumpus hounds wouldn't even have licked them.

I became flexible—against my nature. I went to Burger King to get Whoppers for dinner. It was a lesson for me in how not to impress my mother-in-law with my culinary abilities, and to impress her with my flexibility. We all laughed about it—bringing our firstborn son into the world with a magnificent fast-food delicacy.

Who among us can control our fates with any precision? What do we do when we come to our senses and need to reverse course—or chart a new one?

Shepherd says that we can be quitters or go-getters. As go-getters, we move on, flexibly, paying attention for opportunities, doing the best we can in the circumstances that befall us, and remaining aware of our faults so we minimize the grief to others. There will always be Bumpus hounds in the world. But there will also be Asian restaurants—even on Christmas Day. Such places are ducky opportunities to create wonderful memories.

# CHAPTER 4

# Watch Out for Bullies

**B**ullies will always be among us. They come in many stripes and sizes, kids and adults, solo and in packs. Some bullies fight with words and others with fists and weapons. A real bully can even frighten us simply with a mean look. Jean Shepherd believed that we have to deal with them appropriately. His life lesson in *A Christmas Story* is for us to watch out for bullies.

In the movie, the two bullies, Scut Farkus and Grover Dill, are prototypical baddies. Farkus could bully others on his own—like a sole practitioner, for income tax purposes. But he wants someone such as Dill, whom Shep calls a "cunning little toady," to serve on his crew. Dill offers his green teeth to the mix of menacing nonverbal messages. Scut even bullies Dill in order to form his underling into Farkus' own image of a spooky belligerent. Dill also adds hope that Scut can one day form a movement of bullies, a gang of sycophant combatants. Bullies often run in packs.

Bullies add an abnormal but insuppressible diversity to the world. As Shep puts it, "You were either a bully, a toady, or one of the nameless rabble of victims." That's a thought-provoking way to look at the world! It fits with Shepherd's view of the impact of bullies in both personal and international relations.

## Will Bullies Always Be with Us?

Shepherd and I talked a lot about bullies because he believed we can't live wisely in our imperfect world unless we learn how to deal with them. In *A Christmas Story*, Shepherd portrays neighborhood bullies as a metaphor for verbal and physical bullies at all times and places, and at every level of society, governments included.

There are many social and psychological theories about what transforms someone into a tyrant. In Shepherd's worldview, bullies simply exist. Their origins are often inexplicable; not all bullies come from bully-producing families. The question is how we should handle them.

Ralphie's younger brother, Randy, represents one approach: Fall over and act like a slug. It was easy for him in his winter outfit, wrapped up so tightly and so thoroughly that he couldn't even raise or lower his protruding arms. To pick a fight with Randy was not worth the trouble, anyway. Given his strict uniform, he was a Mom-mandated pacifist.

We all could act like slugs if we're around bullies. When it comes to physical fighting, I've always been a slug. The problem with this approach is that some bullies are so mean they might even pick on slug-like people who are laying low, just minding their own business. Being a slug works best when there are other potential victims who offer at least a modicum of feistiness. Defense in numbers, of sorts.

Scut and his pushy partner, Dill, however, are impossible to ignore in Ralphie's neighborhood. They are aggressive, mean-spirited persons, traveling the yards, scouting for potential targets. They are modern-day desperadoes seeking weaklings to intimidate. They find purpose in life by being cruel toward others and, sometimes, even toward each other. Dill gets annoyed with Farkus, who persistently punches him in the shoulder, perhaps a sign of mock comradeship, but certainly an indication of a pecking order. Farkus needs to ensure that Dill recognizes that Farkus is in charge. Bullies don't like competition, especially from other bullies. Farkus rules like an authoritarian leader of his own neighborhood nation.

During his early adult years, Shepherd was politically liberal—even to the point of helping to form a chapter of a very progressive student group on a university campus. But gradually Shepherd changed politically, becoming more conservative, perhaps even libertarian. He advocated for the checks and balances formalized in the U.S. Constitution, worrying about what would happen without them. He grew concerned about authoritarianism worldwide. He didn't like governments, local or national, telling citizens how to live, but he strongly supported law and order.

For Shepherd, everyday neighborhood bullies were like national and international tyrants; the former could lead to the latter—and often did. Soviet autocrat Joseph Stalin was one of the greatest personal and political bullies of all time. Even his closest colleagues couldn't trust him; he killed many of them without a pinch of conscience. Stalinists frightened Shepherd.

In *A Christmas Story*, Shepherd aimed to address his broader concerns about bullies both personally and on the world stage. Scut represents a tyrannical leader, not just an everyday cruel person. To understand this, we have to dip into the period of the Cold War, when Shepherd began developing his bully-story motif.

Shepherd's midadulthood occurred during the 1950s and '60s, the early part of the Cold War (1947–91) between the United States and the Soviet Union. Tensions were high. Communication between the two superpowers was poor. Diplomacy was nonexistent. Fear of nuclear attack was widespread.

I recall in grade school in the 1950s practicing where to go in the building (avoid windows) and how to posture our bodies on the floor, under our desks, in case of nuclear attack. Today, it seems ludicrous, but back in the fear-inducing Cold War era it was an accepted part of American life. Most Americans saw the difference between good and evil forces in the world quite starkly.

Shepherd closely paid attention to the superpowers' public rhetoric, especially through newspaper accounts (he read news voraciously, clipping stories of interest and eventually using them as fodder for his tales, however exaggerated or reformulated). In his view at the time, the Soviet Union and the United States might indeed challenge each other militarily. And the scariest of the two powers, the Soviet Union, was controlled by volatile dictators (bullies).

Nikita Khrushchev, the first secretary of the Communist Party in the Soviet Union, reportedly even banged his fist and allegedly his shoe on a table at a United Nations General Assembly meeting in 1960. Observers said that the Soviet leader was angry about "wretched capitalists"—including the United States. In Shepherd's mind, these kinds of heated Soviet leaders were bullies with lethal power in the form of advanced nuclear weapons.

In the movie, the whole Farkus affair represents the broader problem of international relations, nuclear war and all. Although the connection between Farkus and the Soviet Union is symbolic, it's played out amazingly well. Scut's "red" (symbolizing communism) fox-fur cap (like a coonskin cap) is meant to be Sovietish, the kind of deep winter clothing worn in Siberia. And Scut's yellow eyes? The Russian blue cat is born with striking yellow eyes. Moreover, Russian pilots were sometimes referred to as the "yellow-eyed" because of their colored goggles. Canadian actor Zack Ward, who played Farkus so wonderfully, actually has green eyes.

The most amazing aspect of the symbolism in this bully-based drama is the name "Scut Farkus." First, bullies create a real fracas; it's their nature. Second, the name "Farkus" is from the Hungarian word for "wolf." When Scut first appears in the movie, the music is from "Peter and the Wolf."

## Where Did Shepherd Get the Name "Scut"?

"Scut," an unusual name, is taken partly from the Scud Missile System, a tactical ballistic system developed by the Soviet Union during the Cold War. The name "Scud" came from a NATO report developed by Western intelligence agencies. The missiles were employed for decades and continue to be used in modern versions. Shepherd loved the nasty sound of "Scut."

Shepherd was always brilliant in naming his characters—though not always as obvious as we might like. One more thing about "Scut" demonstrates this: It's also a Middle English term that refers to a speedy runner. Scud missiles were launched from trucks that could be moved around quickly, making it difficult for the enemy to locate and destroy them (like Scut and Grover running around Ralphie's neighborhood, appearing out of nowhere, even upside down, hanging from a playground bar).

I'm struck today, when I see authoritarian leaders in news reports, that they are usually pictured amid a batch of military-clad, male underlings. These are apparently the Dills of our age, the true-blue toadies who uncomplainingly do whatever their dictator wishes. I can imagine a tyrannical leader punching one of the toadies in the shoulder and telling him to stay loyal to the cause of intimidation.

Shepherd said publicly on a few occasions that *A Christmas Story* is an antiwar and even an anti-gun movie. Actually, he had a far more nuanced understanding of war and weapons based on his anti-totalitarian views and on his related fears about a nuclear war during the period when he developed the Red Ryder BB-rifle story. Shepherd opposed putting weapons in the hands of bullies with low self-esteem and delusions of authoritarian grandeur—like Scut Farkus and Grover Dill.

Shepherd said to me that we need to beware of all bullies and their toadies. A demented toady might even be the first one to fire a nuclear rocket or missile—like a snowball. The irony of Dill's snowball hitting Ralphie in the eye, by the way, is the fact that everyone was warning Ralphie not to get a Red Ryder BB rifle for fear that he would shoot his own eye out. Dill got to Ralphie first, as Scut cheered him on.

It makes sense to avoid such bullies, as Ralphie and his pals try to do, and as I learned growing up. Often, even mild verbal confrontation will fuel latent animosities and lead to physical skirmishes.

A strange mental defect among tried and true bullies, however, is that they don't understand that there will always be others who can take them out. They naïvely think they are invincible. Ralphie taught Scut otherwise by beating him up.

When I was a kid, I was walking down the sidewalk and the local persecutor, Jimmy, descended upon me with a fightin' look in his eyes. Unlike Dill and Farkus, he never uttered anything; I wondered if he was capable of speech. He started swinging his arms side to side and charging toward me at the same time. Now that I look back on it, his swinging-while-running routine seems funny because it slowed him down. It's not a very sustainable form of multitasking. Imagine a top Olympic runner swinging his arms while competing in the 400-meter dash.

I took off for home, full speed. I was not going to ask him what he had on his mind. I knew. I was about to get pounded. As I rounded the turn into my backyard, I saw my nine-year-older brother, smoking a Lucky Strike cigarette. Jimmy soon came around the corner behind me and stopped in his muddy tracks. He looked at my brother, who flicked his butt at Jimmy. My 6'5", size-15-shoed, pure-muscled brother—later nicknamed "Bigfoot"—could have laid Jimmy low with one blow. The surprised bully ceased waving his arms, turned around, and took off for home. That was my last personal encounter with Jimmy even though he continued to terrorize the neighborhood.

According to Shepherd, the best life lesson about bullies is to beware of them—and avoid them, if possible. They are nearly always itching for a fight. They don't play fair. They don't care about social rules. They have no interest in keeping the peace; they are trying to uproot the social decorum that enables us all to live together in relative harmony.

Yet we do need courageous people in our neighborhoods and in the world who will take on the Dills and Farkuses. Ralphie did it by sheer adrenalin and had to be stopped by Mom from going too far. As Shepherd put it to me, deterrence is not an option; it's a necessity.

My grandson wanted to know when he should fight back against bullies. What if a bully starts hitting him? I had to admit that we must defend ourselves sometimes. We can hope that other rational people are around and will help us do so—such as on a playground; numbers can make a big difference. According to Shepherd, this is why democracies form alliances with each other, against totalitarian nations and their sycophant supporters around the world. In my case, it only took my

4

older brother to convince my local bully to turn around in his tracks, and never return to my yard again.

In Ralphie's case, however, he was both surprised by Dill's snowball and already in a very bad mood. He was despondent about receiving a low grade on his theme regarding what he wanted for Christmas—an assignment which he saw as the route to getting his current life dream, the Red Ryder BB rifle. Ralphie was vulnerable to his own emotional outburst. Bullies should beware of pushing good people too far.

## Was Ralphie Sorry for Losing His Temper with Scut?

As Shepherd makes clear in the story, Ralphie had simply "gone out of his skull" for a few minutes, pounding Scut bloody. After the fight, however, Ralphie realizes that he has lost his temper and acted irrationally. He cries uncontrollably when Mom arrives and pulls him off of Scut. According to Shepherd, in order to sanely assess bullies' actual threats, we also have to manage our own emotional states.

Ralphie could have accepted Dill's snowball, wiped the snow and ice from his eyes, and walked away. He didn't need to lie down like a slug or engage in military action. Usually, the best course is to head home or to another place of safety, like inside school. That's the life lesson I tried to share with my grandson. It was the best I could do, given the seemingly endless challenge of living in a world with bullies. Then again, I am more of a lover than a fighter—or just a chicken. Hardly a bigfoot.

## CHAPTER 5

# Don't Shoot Your Eye Out

You'll shoot your eye out!" is Google's most searched term related to *A Christmas Story*. The phrase is even a folk rule in its own right. And it's hard to imagine a parent—at least a mother—who has not proclaimed a version of the warning when one of her kids asks about getting a slingshot or a BB gun.

Of course, the oft-repeated warning is fired at Ralphie on his quest to convince adults to help him acquire a Red Ryder rifle for Christmas. He has got to keep ducking the verbal shots, each one more disheartening to the poor kid than the previous one. He's worried about not getting equipped to shoot the evil Black Bart and other desperadoes, whereas the adults seem to be more concerned with keeping him from acquiring his knurled-stocked beauty.

When Ralphie accidentally blurts out to Mom what he truly wants for Christmas—the rifle—Mom becomes the first one in the movie to issue the depressing warning. Ralphie knew she would be unhappy with his heart's desire, but he's caught off guard, like an anxious dog yelping in response to the doorbell. Ralphie has no choice but to try to walk back his request, pretending he was just kidding. He says he really wants some Tinker Toys. Sure—he can throw them like spears at Bart. Good luck with that plan, Ralphie. If desperadoes are truly trolling Cleveland Street, you need a real, scary weapon—preferably with a "thing that tells time."

Ironically, Ralphie calls the "classic mother BB-gun block" a "deadly phrase." Then he soldiers on, claiming that "Flick is getting one" for Christmas—as if he knows what Flick's parents are planning. He's trying to lay a guilt trip on Mom. Doesn't she love Ralphie the way Flick's mother loves him? Not a good salvo, Ralphie. Mom can see right through it. "BB guns are dangerous," warns Mom. "I don't want anybody shooting his eye out." Obviously, she means Flick too; she seems to be an early supporter of local BB-gun control. Ralphie expected her recalcitrance, but the verbal volleys are still tough for him to hear.

Ralphie's Plan B is Miss Shields, his teacher. He figures he can write a knockout theme paper for her about what he wants for Christmas. She will listen. She isn't compromised by maternal instincts. But after receiving his disappointing theme grade back from Miss Shields, Ralphie reads on his paper exactly what he heard from Mom: "You'll shoot your eye out!" Ouch! That raw shot really hurts. It's Ralphie's second purple heart.

Ralphie's explanation for the repeated warning drips with kid fantasy: "My mother must have gotten to Miss Shields. There could be no other explanation." Ralphie even imagines Mom and Miss Shields as a pair of witches, chanting, "You'll shoot your eye out." In Ralphie's mind, the two-person warning is now a conspiracy—a clear sign of "irrational prejudice." It's hard to battle a contrary clutch of collaborators.

Finally, Ralphie charges to his last, ultimate resort for a fair hearing—Santa, who adjudicates all allegedly good-or-bad behavior. Besides, Santa is a man; he will understand Ralphie's predicament and deliver the goods. But Ralphie doesn't receive a favorable legal finding. Santa fires the same shot-in-the-eye warning at Ralphie, just before pushing him down  the slide with a "Ho, ho, ho!" Ralphie's three petitions to adults have all been rejected based on the same conspiratorial plot. Ralphie seems to be mortally wounded in his quest for the gun of all guns.

But immediately afterward, at the base of the slide, the Old Man reminds Ralphie that Santa knows the real score when it comes to Christmas gifts. "Don't worry," says the Old Man. "He [Santa] knows." Of course, the Old Man knows; he already bought or will purchase the rifle for Ralphie, unbeknownst to Mom.

Still, the warning stands out in the movie, repeated for memorable effect in the film's major plotline. The movie's protagonist, Ralphie, is blocked in his quest to become a protector of the neighborhood. Of course, if Ralphie does secure a rifle, he might indeed shoot himself. Santa is a bit of a jerk, but Mom and Miss Shields are wise counselors who truly care about the flighty kids under their wings.

Worried about their own little beavers ("Little Beaver" was the Red Ryder's young companion), Mom and Miss Shields get this bigger picture. They are in the child-nurturing business. Santa is just a naysaying nitwit, anxious to get out of his Santa suit and go out for a drink.

## Do We All "Shoot Our Eyes Out"?

From the perspective of parable-teller Jean Shepherd, the eye-shot warning is figurative. It's not just about kids accidentally shooting themselves. In fact, it's not even merely about weapons. "You'll shoot your eye out!" is a cautionary expression about the human condition. Unless we are careful, every one of us might "shoot" ourselves, with words as well as actions. We dwell in a messy world filled with unforeseen challenges and unknown consequences that call for careful actions.

Shepherd's life lesson is that we need to be aware of the potential consequences of our decisions and corresponding actions. Everything we say and do has potential risks. Are we aware of such consequences? Have we considered them? If so, are we prepared for them? In short, are we being wise, conscientious people? Or are we simply doing what we want now, without carefully looking forward in life?

"Don't shoot your eye out!" is a call to be responsible—to approach the future with careful deliberation, counting the potential costs as well as benefits of turning our desires into real actions. There is no major problem with Ralphie pursuing his dream; he's honing his persuasive skills along the way and learning that he can't get everything he wants in life. But what if his dream becomes a reality?

Shepherd believed that we all need to be careful because, as we pursue people and things in life, we might just find that the results are not what we expected. We don't fully consider the potential cost to others as well as ourselves. Often, we don't even listen to those who are trying to help us be cautious. Mom, Miss Shields, and perhaps even the crusty Santa are simply providing some due diligence for the dreamy Ralphie: "Ralphie, do you really know how to be a responsible owner of a weapon? Do you have any idea what you're getting into?"

In other words, Shepherd used the warning about "shooting ourselves" figuratively. We humans sometimes march ahead in life without considering the likelihood of getting wounded on the battlefield. He said it was similar to going into debt by buying many things we don't really need. Before long, the credit card interest payments are shooting us in the foot; we can't buy even the basics for life. Or we dream about a pet and finally get a cute puppy, but then realize that we don't have the time or space to care for it well. We also let down friends, family, or business partners, creating ill will.

Sometimes, we nearly shoot our eyes out because we are so narrowly and naïvely focused on solving a legitimate problem. Blind to the potential consequences of our actions, we charge ahead anyway. And we don't seek counsel or listen to unsolicited advice.

I was frustrated by an invasion of aphids in a locust tree over our backyard patio. When I sat on the peaceful patio to enjoy a pleasant summer evening, the aphids dropped on me like tiny green snowflakes. They got in my hair, down my shirt, in my pockets—everywhere. When I tried catching or swatting them, they squished into bits of green goo.

I was determined to get rid of the tiny bugs. I made a plan when I discovered that lacewings love to eat aphids. Aha! I just needed lacewings. I was making progress, smartly using science to improve my lot in life. I was becoming a savvy land manager, heading up my own department of natural resources—or was I?

I ordered a package of hundreds of cute little lacewings. When they arrived, I climbed a ladder into the tree to release the delicate, soft-winged insects that look like tiny hang gliders. It was magic. In minutes, the lacewings ascended from their prison box to lacewing heaven—a green smorgasbord of their favorite buffet. Soon they were flying all over the tree, gobbling up aphids like they were chewing on chicken wings. I felt like a real nature hero. I had returned our backyard to a touch of the garden of Eden. I slept well.

For a couple of days.

Then disaster struck (as it often does in *A Christmas Story*). Blue jays began arriving en masse to chow down on the lacewings. Blue jays! Among the noisiest, most belligerent of all birds. They called their kin from blocks away to join the party: "All you can eat!"

I had inadvertently opened a fast-food restaurant for the rowdy birds, who were fighting among themselves for control of the tree. Flocks of them were yacking all day long. I couldn't even take a nap. And I really enjoy afternoon snoozes.

Worse yet was the poop. The bird dung was white with black blobs of stringy balls, drooping like tears and then plopping on the patio and anyone sitting below.

I had lost the battle for control of critters in the locust tree. I could only wait for the raucous birds to finish gorging themselves on my lovely little mail-order lacewings. It took a few, miserable days. Then, as the blue jays departed, the aphids returned, regrouping on the undersides of leaves, consuming chow from their own menu.

I eventually learned to coexist with my tiny green neighbors. I purchased a sizable patio umbrella. When I was bored, I could sit directly under it and watch the aphids fall from the air and then slide off the umbrella edges. Cheap entertainment.

Yes, I shot myself with a seemingly wonderful plan.

This narrowness of vision is Ralphie's issue. He has trouble thinking through the possible ramifications of owning and using a BB rifle. He's caught in the dreamy goal of chasing off bad guy Black Bart and company. Using even a BB gun responsibly requires much more than a good intention. Shooting at a metal target is a bad idea!

## What Is Ralphie's Real Education?

Shepherd loved to tease me about the problem of academic "overshoot" by professors such as myself; he said that we academicians claim to know more than we really do. He believed that there are two kinds of education—schooling and life. If we don't have enough life experience, no amount of the formal instruction will keep us from shooting our eyes out. We all need real-life experience, often learned from and modeled by others, such as parents and older siblings. And we need to reflect on our own life trials and errors. Ralphie is getting quite an education in the movie—and not just via the classroom with Miss Shields.

In fact, taking care of anything in our lives necessitates more than a right motive. So does controlling the aphids—if they should be controlled. Aphids are not even summerlong inhabitants. I, a professor, overshot.

Shepherd tied the "You'll shoot your eye out!" warning to his more sinister parable about bullies and nuclear war. He believed that the good guys might mistakenly be the first ones to fire on the bad guys. Lacking adequate knowledge, assuming they have more "intelligence" than they actually do, the good guys could fire at a mistakenly perceived threat. The worldwide consequences could be catastrophic.

Good guys and bad guys—in everyday life as in war—can fail to gain enough knowledge of themselves and their situations to be able to act wisely. Warnings alone are insufficient; we also need wisdom.

The great aphid disaster taught me this lesson—"in spades," as Shepherd used to say. The old bridge card game adage means that we need to know the strength of our hand. Do we really have great cards to play in the game of life? Or are we overconfident, setting ourselves up to shoot our eye out? Just release a box of lacewings in a tree in your yard and then try to take a peaceful nap.

# CHAPTER 6

## Care for Family

**M**om wants Randy to stay warm on the way to school. She thoroughly bundles him up to protect him from the harsh winter weather. But the poor kid can barely move. He walks like a penguin and wobbles like a bowling pin. His arms protrude outward, limiting his reach in other directions. His scarf covers his mouth, making it difficult for others to hear him cry for help when he needs it. Shep says that Randy looks like a "tick about to pop."

Mom says, after struggling for a while to wrap up Randy at home one morning, that he will just have to wait to get to school to put his arms down—even though it seems that he might have to go to the bathroom as well. I can recall as a kid peeing in my pants at home after school because I couldn't get my snowsuit off quickly enough even with my mother's help.

When a couple of kids pass Randy on the school route, one of them intentionally knocks him down. Randy rolls back and forth on the frigid ground, unable to get up. He half cries and half screams to Ralphie for help. Ralphie, realizing Randy's plight, asks Flick to "wait up" so he can go back and get his brother. Ralphie cares about Randy, especially in such a desperate condition. He knows that this is what siblings do for one another. He's going to take care of Randy, just as he would want help if he were the younger sibling.

*A Christmas Story* offers a life lesson about being family members who care for one another amid many challenges. The more I watch the film, the more I especially appreciate the care that Ralphie and Randy display toward one another. Mom is the primary nurturer in the Parker family, but the brothers are mutually caring as well.

For instance, a significant part of the movie shows the Parker brothers and Ralphie's friends in the snow, navigating between home and school. Randy is not quite old enough to have his own friends to join him during these weekday journeys. Ralphie needs to watch over his younger sibling, as he did when Randy was intentionally knocked over.

During the fight between Ralphie and bully Scut Farkus, Ralphie gets so emotional that he loses all sense of proportion—physically and verbally. Randy witnesses Ralphie pounding the daylights out of Scut, revealing what is probably a new perspective for Randy on his otherwise mild-mannered brother. Randy also hears Ralphie uttering strings of profanity and obscenity that might rival the Old Man's furnace-war bravado. But what can Randy do? How can he be the kind of caring brother that Ralphie tries to be for him? Randy, too, feels called to be a caring member of the Parker clan.

## Why Show the Kids Going to and from School?

Shepherd told me that humans live by everyday rituals—like driving to work and walking or taking the bus to school. He wanted to capture the rituals of childhood that storytellers typically ignore, such as sharing family meals, writing school papers, unwrapping presents, sparring verbally, and traversing to and from the local school. Also, the conversations along the path between home and school contribute to the various plotlines. Ralphie, in particular, has two "families"—the Parker family and his group of pals. The school path and the Parker table are Ralphie's two primary places of "family" drama.

Randy finds Ralphie's eyeglasses in the snow. This is important because later the Old Man complains at the dinner table about Ralphie having potentially lost his glasses again. Glasses were not cheap. Worse yet, losing one's glasses signaled to parents a kind of irresponsibility, even though it was easy to misplace them. Keeping track of one's glasses was an important task.

Also, Randy manages to pick up the glasses without falling over and getting stranded sluglike in the snow once again; he knows that he must get home safely to secure help for his brother. With all the racket going on as Ralphie pummels Scut, probably no one would hear Randy's typical, pathetic cries for help: "Come on, guys, pick me up! Pick me up!"

Randy finds Ralphie's glasses and heads home with them, running as best he can in his full penguin regalia. Randy thereby becomes an important messenger for his brother's well-being. Randy is Paul Revere, shuffling along in the dimming sunlight to the Parker cottage to alert

Mom that Ralphie is in deep trouble; the bullies have come and Ralphie is battling one of them. I wish that Randy's report to Mom had been depicted in the film. I wonder which was worse, in Randy's eyes, the fisticuffs or the swearing?

Mom arrives at the snowy battlefield and pries her oldest son off of the bloodied bully, who then glances around in embarrassment. Mom doesn't look after Scut, the known neighborhood tormenter; he can fend for himself, while Mom, Ralphie, and Randy safely return home. Of course, Schwartz and Flick have already run off; maybe they worried that they might face bully retaliation.

## Who Forgot the "Idiot Strings"?

Of course, the actor playing Ralphie (Peter Billingsley) does not really slug the actor (Zack Ward) playing the chief bully, Scut. We see the fight from an angle that only makes it look like Ralphie is pounding on Scut. One problem: Ralphie's mittens were attached to his coat with old-fashioned "idiot strings" so he wouldn't lose them and so he looked more authentic for the period. Each time Ralphie pretended to swing at Scut, however, poor Ward would get a rebound blow from a frozen mitten.

Randy knows that Mom has seen Ralphie walloping Scut, but also that she has overheard Ralphie delivering a rich stream of kid-forbidden language. Shep describes young Ralphie's language during the fight, "I have since heard of people under extreme duress, speaking in strange tongues. I became conscious that a steady torrent of obscenities and swearing of all kinds was pouring out of me as I screamed." How would Mom deal with Ralphie on that issue? Presumably worse than she did over Ralphie's single F-bomb uttered during the father-son, tire-change episode. This new infraction would require much more penitence than sucking on a bar of Lifebuoy soap.

Unsurprisingly, Randy is troubled by the whole verbal-physical affair. He takes refuge in the cabinet under the kitchen sink, fearful of what will happen when the Old Man arrives home from work. There is not much more Randy can do for Ralphie, except maybe hope and pray for the least-harsh punishment. He must feel relieved, though, when he sees Mom return the glasses to Ralphie after the Old Man asks Ralphie if he lost the spectacles. Randy has done a splendid deed for his sibling.

When the Parker family heads to Higbee's department store for the encounter with Santa Claus and his creepy minions, the parents hope to sneak in some last-minute shopping without their offspring. They leave Ralphie and Randy alone so the brothers can get in line for the stairway-to-Santa expedition. Mom asks Ralphie to look after Randy, like an older sibling should: "Take Randy's hand and hold on to him." The Old Man confirms the message as a stronger command: "Yeah, stay together, don't get lost."

Ralphie seems to temporarily forget his mission and starts to walk away without grabbing Randy's hand. Who wants to be seen in public holding the hand of a little brother, anyway? Ralphie is thinking about what he needs to say to Santa—how to make his pitch—so a bit of forgetfulness is understandable.

Ralphie turns back, gloms on to Randy's hand and tries to size up the wild scene with all of the shoppers, elves, and other characters rushing around and bumping into one another. Is this what Christmas is really all about—frenetic last-minute spending and outlandish adult make-believe? Also, the guy dressed in the Santa outfit is booming "Ho, ho, ho" like a stranded mountaineer, across the Alps, his weary voice carrying above the noisy crowd and holiday music. Is the guy playing Santa actually the arbiter of good and bad behavior, the final judge of who gets what for Christmas?

## Did Ralphie Believe That Santa Was a Fake?

Shepherd told me that Ralphie presumes the guy playing Santa is a fake, and that the red nose suggests that Santa has been imbibing a bit of holiday cheer, probably right at his throne. Moreover, Ralphie is not a true believer in Santa. But Ralphie is willing to try anything in his quest for the Red Ryder rifle. What if, by remote chance, the rotund guy on the hill really does know if kids have been naughty or nice? What if he somehow influences who gets what for Christmas? At this stage in the story for Ralphie, it's best not to question—but to believe. When facing Santa, there is no room for agnosticism or atheism. Shepherd also compared going up the mountain to see Santa to "stepping up" to a church confessional—pretty scary, especially for a kid—but also a matter of "faith."

Ralphie hangs on tightly to Randy's hand, partly because two people are stronger than one. They will navigate together through the noise and crowd, the sheer unpredictability of the Christmas chaos. The stairway up to the booming Santa looks forbidding. The exit slide is not a short, playground variety; it's two stories high and looks like one at a big theme park. The two-story slide was acquired from a swimming pool company.

Adults surely like their dramatic holiday cheer; the whole first floor of Higbee's is like a stage with real-life characters and sets everywhere. Ralphie is trying to fit in unnoticed, with Randy at his side, almost under his wing. We can only guess how spooked Randy is by the chaos. But we also see that he trusts Ralphie to lead him around and protect him from strange-looking characters.

I remember being afraid to see Santa in person when I was young, and I have a photo to prove it. Sitting on Santa's lap, I appear to be completely dazed and confused, not delighted and hopeful about which gifts I might receive. I recall wearing my long woolen coat and winter, rancher-styled hat—and, of course, my black galoshes. This clanking fashion of the day, because we often left them unbuckled, were always too tight to fall off our feet, anyway, and they collected snow that melted and was drinkable when we became thirsty out on the neighborhood snow trails. But most of all, I remember that I didn't like the look and voice of Santa, and I didn't want to be there; I probably cried right after the photo. Distress takes many forms for kids.

Ralphie and Randy head to the line. They must confer about gifts with the top influencer on the mountain before Santa leaves for the night. The powers that be have announced on the public address system that the store is closing.

Only one immediate problem: The brothers are not really at the beginning of the snaky lineup to the mountain steps to see Santa. A scary adult man, well dressed in a fancy hat and coat, shouts, "Young man." Ralphie realizes that the stranger is talking to him. Oh, boy, what's next? The guy continues, "Hey, kid. Just where do you think you're going?"

Ralphie is beginning to realize that he's doing something wrong. It's embarrassing. Frightening. Confusing. Ralphie is once again lost in a bewildering adult world. He tells the man he's just "going up to see Santa." Then the boisterous guy proclaims to Ralphie, above the din, "The line *ends* here. It begins *there*."

Oh, no! The official-looking man points far back in the store, to the real start of the line.

Ralphie gets himself and his brother safely to the correct spot in line, but then more bedlam ensues in this season of peace and love. First, an odd-looking kid in flight goggles shows up next to them, telling Ralphie in a strange tone, "I like Santa." Then come the Wizard of Oz characters.

It's a veritable circus of costumed people who seem to have nothing to do with the real meaning of Christmas. And these characters all act like it's okay to pester people who are there just to conduct essential business with Santa. Ralphie becomes the responsible spokesperson for the brotherly pair, telling everyone else to get lost, more or less; he's a bit intimidated, but he won't give an inch for the pair—verbally or physically. After all, Ralphie is on a critical, two-pronged mission—to protect Randy from the waves of odd people and to make his personal case to Santa for the Red Ryder rifle.

## Does Screenwriter Shepherd Himself Appear in the Movie?

The man who tells Ralphie to go to the back of the line at Higbee's is none other than the screenwriter, Jean Shepherd. Behind him, after a child, is his wife, Leigh Brown—who is also given a screenwriter credit for the movie. Of course, Shepherd's actual voice is heard throughout the movie as the adult Ralphie.

The witch comes by and calls Ralphie a "tasty little boy." I probably would have stomped on her pointed little tootsies and told her to bug off. But Ralphie takes the more peaceful approach of informing her that he's busy "thinking." Director Bob Clark had sprung the witch on poor Ralphie without the actor, Peter Billingsley, knowing it would happen. Ralphie *is* thinking about how to respond! He has got to prepare his legal brief for the arbiter of gift-giving in the red-felt hat with white trim and pom-pom tassel. Ralphie needs to make his BB-gun pleading as if it's the most important hearing on earth, before the U.S. Supreme Court, with no chance for appeal.

Randy first must go through the Santa-and-elves pretrial appearance. Ralphie can't leave him behind. Ralphie sees how nasty the first elf, the kid-traffic cop, is to Randy. She proclaims impatiently, "Listen, little boy, we got a lot of people waiting here, so get going." Now, Ralphie is worrying even more about Randy and himself. What have they gotten into—all in the name of pitching Santa on their presents? When the other elf tosses Randy down the slide like a sack of potatoes, Ralphie visually follows his little brother's trajectory momentarily to make sure Randy lands safely, free of major injuries.

There are undoubtedly times when Ralphie gets a bit frustrated about having to take care of Randy. Do any siblings get along perfectly, especially when they are young? But Ralphie is on top of things during this escapade to Santa's heavenly realm, even with Ralphie's own complicated rhetorical mission to confront Santa face-to-face.

Ralphie finally makes it through the Higbee's-Santa chaos with Randy. Mom and the Old Man meet them at the bottom of the slide. They have survived, although Ralphie wishes he had made his case for the rifle more successfully; he freaked out at the last minute and let Santa intimidate him into first asking just for a football—truly a great winter present in northern Indiana, where every field is covered with snow and ice and you have to try throwing the ball while wearing mittens.

Shepherd told me that one of the things adults don't always understand about being a kid is all of the confusing events and people that are a natural part of being a grown-up. To children, the adult world is like a maze of confusing rules and rituals. It's not always clear whom to trust and how to act. Even a simple thing like getting in line at a hectic store can cause anxiety. When a parent or older sibling can lead the way, the bewilderment is not so emotionally difficult. Ralphie is a hero to Randy.

*A Christmas Story* shows that family members are called to look after each other. Siblings who care for one another in times of need are a gift. And as we get older, we can laugh together at the ways we previously treated one another—for good and sometimes less so. It appears to me that Ralphie and Randy are well on the way to a lifetime of good memories peppered with plenty of family laughs. There will be mutual blessings which they can now taste and will get to savor in the years ahead. Together, they have crossed one of life's formidable mountains, safely to the other side, where they met the rest of the waiting family.

# CHAPTER 7

# Tackle Your Technology

The Old Man hears something strange in the house. Is it a burglar? Or maybe the Bumpus hounds scratching at the door?

The Old Man says, "Shh."

The Parker family listens intently. But what does the superattentive master of the house actually hear?

He exclaims, "Aha! Aha! It's a clinker! That blasted stupid furnace . . ."

Thus ensues one of the most famous basement battle scenes in the history of moviedom.

Yet we never actually see the Old Man's nemesis, the cellar furnace. Nor do we witness the trenchant battles themselves! We just hear them taking place in the frightening underworld.

All we can observe and nearly smell are the battle effects—sooty smoke rising upstairs from the under-the-floor battle scene, along with ashes dusted on the Old Man's face and plastered on his garb when he retreats upstairs after each skirmish.

## Why Did Shepherd Focus the Old Man's Attention on the Furnace?

Shepherd believed that the perfect way in *A Christmas Story* to begin addressing the technological aspects of human life was with the once-ubiquitous coal-fired home furnace. In Shepherd's view, old and new technologies will always be with us. There is no going back to primitive living—at least for most people who get a taste of modern life. Even the survivor-style TV shows are a farce, with characters actually surrounded by crews and equipment to document the "real" nature scenes. The old furnace represents the ancient-but-enduring battle between human and machine.

Today, we think of technologies as electronic devices. But all around us, throughout our cities and homes, are additional, frustrating low-tech gadgets such as leaky plumbing faucets, malfunctioning auto trunk openers, intermittent doorbells, and finicky garage door openers. And every Christmas we must do battle with the tiny lights on trees and wreaths; at least in the Old Man's day, you could easily spot and replace the large, burned-out incandescent bulbs.

What about our modern, high-tech devices, such as computers and mobile phones? It's hard to distinguish sometimes between a feature, a bug, and death. And what about artificial intelligence (AI)? Shepherd would likely say that all intelligence is somewhat artificial, whether created by machines or people.

*A Christmas Story* captures an important life lesson: We have to tackle our technologies. If we don't keep them under control, they will bring us down. The man-machine battle is an age-old war that neither side can completely win. Technologies are formidable opponents in life, not simply signs of human progress. We ignore that truth at our own peril.

Shepherd said that all technological devices are man-made sources of frustration—sooner or later. The technologies change, but our related annoyances persist, and can quickly escalate. The Old Man could buy a new coal furnace, but he would probably still suffer the chronic clinkers. The same for his pile-of-junk Olds. If he buys a shiny new car, it will eventually have its own problems.

Even the sound of the word "clinker" suggests something nefarious. One of the best-known, stereotypical "clinking" sounds in movies is prison inmates running their metal cups along prison cell bars. The Old Man's cellar is one of his battlegrounds—or his jails.

Old coal-fired furnaces demonstrated a recurring problem that had to be addressed by someone in the house who was willing to do battle periodically. The problem—a clinker—was caused by a combination of incorrect furnace settings and cheap coal. You had to have just the right amount of air and quality coal for continuous, high-temperature combustion. Otherwise, noncombustible lumps of residue would form (clinkers) and fall onto the boiler floor, making a racket. The Old Man could hear them falling miles away; his ears had been tuned to the sound over decades of careful eavesdropping on the emerging clinkers in his own low-tech crypt.

Moreover, Shepherd had an interesting view of technologies as "living" problems. Obviously, none of us fully controls our technologies. Gadgets seem to have their own lives. Often, they do what they want, according to some mysterious, internal will to perform or malfunction. We create technologies, but then they take on a life of their own.

Shepherd told me that every technology offers only short-term pleasure. They die, just as we do. Or we get a new one, like a facelift. We put our hopes in the latest models, and then move on when they no longer please us.

Shepherd and I talked cars, probably his strongest personal interest after storytelling. He loved Volkswagens, but told me that if I bought one in the winter in Michigan, I would already hear it rusting as I drove off the new-car lot. He jokingly said he appreciated my full-size Chevy station wagon because it made him feel like we were maneuvering around in a military truck, which he drove years ago while in the service.

## Will Humans Ever Overcome Technologies?

Shepherd wondered why people get so enamored with technologies, including preferring one imperfect *brand* (or "personality") of devices to others. In Shepherd's view, this is a perennial issue, probably pondered throughout human history, beginning with technologies like flints, used to start fires. Being human means constantly battling technologies that have their own, imperfect personalities. It also means believing that one type (or brand) of technology is superior even if it, too, is defective.

Technologies tend to create our dependence on experts to fix them. But in Shepherd's view, men (more than women) end up trying to tackle the technologies on their own. Women know better, he claimed.

Men *think* they can fully control technology. And they believe that they can do so without consulting experts or even looking at instruction manuals.

The ongoing battle between man and machine is like a war drama. Shep says that the Old Man was known as a "feared furnace fighter." The Old Man yells "clinker" and jumps into action. The fight is on! It's a never-ending battle between man and machine.

Imagine a battlefield confrontation: "Attention, family! We have a clinker attacking on the right flank! Prepare to engage!" The Old Man, charging into combat with the cry of the low-tech, one-person brigade, flies down the darkly lit basement stairs—tripping on a roller skate and swearing—to take his field position, face-to-face with the dark enemy. He has been called to the domestic military front to tackle what he calls the menacing "pile of junk" (to Shepherd, all technologies at some level are junk).

Unfortunately, his battle will be a temporary victory. Colonel Parker will win skirmishes, but never the war. He's destined in life to try to keep the clinking clunker running with his questionable ammunition (coal) and an untrained lieutenant (Mom) who keeps adjusting the battlefield technologies (the upstairs furnace controls) on him. Meanwhile, the enemy repeatedly outflanks him, clinking without warning.

In the film, we never see the evil behemoth dwelling somewhere in the dark, dank place where monsters hide (as kids imagine in a shadowy, odorous cellar). The Old Man just disappears into the abyss, descending into a lower level of Dante's inferno, a place of diabolical warfare between the mystical forces of good and evil. No one else in the family even wants to peek into that terrifying place, let alone to engage firsthand the devilish behemoth who dwells below.

Shepherd believed that the inner workings of technology will always be somewhat mysterious to us. Except for real experts, who intimately know the "minds" of these machines after years of difficult battles, with physical scars on their hands and emotional wounds in their psyches, we mere mortals live in the elusive realm of technological bewilderment. We respond to recurring and new techno-disasters like green recruits suddenly inserted into the front line of combat after minimal training. If we can find the instruction manual, it's probably indecipherable, anyway—either written only for knowledgeable experts or poorly translated from an extraterrestrial language. We trust the manuals at our own peril even when we must go into battle.

Shepherd believed that technological brands are like religious denominations; many of us can't live with or without particular ones, and they can both please and frustrate us. We have our favorites—Macs or PCs, iPhones or Android devices, a Samsung or a Sony. Technological brands have a cult status. We think that by aligning ourselves with one brand we are better off in life, living the life of "chosen" people, closer to heaven than the heathen who favor other brands.

The way Shepherd put it, the experts serve as our technological "priests," exorcising the clinking demons. We call on them for help, unsure of what kind of mystical ceremony they will engage in to repair it.

The Old Man, however, fantasizing about being a "real man," doesn't need any stinkin' licensed repair experts with certification badges, official uniforms, and special consultations. He will "fix" everything himself, swiftly, impressively.

Yet his lay expertise is never adequate, because techno-problems recur and even morph. The Old Man is destined to technological futility, a war he will never win. It's a messy equivalent to rebooting computers in order to fix underlying problems—magic when it actually works. But even when it does ameliorate the immediate problem, we often don't know why. Our technological understanding is shrouded in mystery.

The Old Man has to tackle comparable technological challenges with his beloved Oldsmobile—another "pile of junk." Ironically, he remains a fanatic about the Olds brand of vehicles. Shepherd believed that none of us likes to admit that our technological purchases were less than stellar; no one will ever say that they bought a lemon, especially right after shoveling out the cash for a shiny, unblemished new one. So, we just pretend that we love every new clunker we purchase, even as we get confused with it and malfunctions begin appearing.

One of my friends hasn't been able to figure out for four years how to reset the clock in his car to and from daylight savings time. "No problem," he says, "I just do the mental conversion." It drives me crazy to be in the car with him. My mind keeps saying, "Fix it!" If I were a computer programmer, I would need weekly therapy sessions.

## Do Cars Have Personalities?

Shepherd was a car aficionado who for a few years was part owner and operator of a foreign car service business in Ohio, where he apparently specialized in Austins and Triumphs. He knew cars well and loved writing columns for *Car and Driver* magazine as well as joining friends at the Indianapolis 500, sometimes even in the pits. To him, every car and each brand of auto has its own living personality. But we'll never truly understand vehicles unless we also understand drivers—a tall order.

Shepherd knew, as represented by the Old Man's auto skirmishes, that vehicles are idols that can seduce us into naïve loyalties. This is why Shep compares auto-brand allegiance to religious loyalties: "Some men are Baptists, others Catholics. My father was an Oldsmobile man." Yet, the Old Man confesses, "That [Olds SOB] would freeze up in the middle of the summer in the equator." It doesn't sound like a blessed icon for personal devotion.

Many apparent technological malfunctions are really user issues. We are the problem. We don't even open, let alone read, the owner's manual; it takes up too much space in the glove compartment and lacks a decent index, anyway. We forget scheduled service—or don't want to pay for it. Who says we need a new "cabin" air filter every six months anyway? We aren't pilots. So what if I replace it every two years? Will the engine explode? I'll just wear one of my old COVID masks when I'm driving; they are taking up room in the glove compartment, anyway—where the manual should be. Plus, wearing one of these facial filters while steering around the city elicits numerous smiles from other drivers; I save money and make their day, showing them that they are smarter than I am.

My wonderfully gifted auto technician, trained in Europe on Italian and German vehicles, regularly showed me, without intending to be critical, that I was the problem—not my car. The most embarrassing example was when I brought in my sedan for the oddest odor, which was getting so bad I couldn't stand being in the car with the windows closed. I told him that something was melting in the engine compartment, probably a hose. I proudly reported that I smelled burning rubber—no doubt about it. Given my excellent clues, he discovered the problem quickly: I had left a plate of fresh shrimp from Costco in the trunk for two weeks during a blistering July. It took a Mercedes-certified expert to help me diagnose that one correctly.

In *A Christmas Story*, the Old Man knows that flat tires need to be tackled regularly. So, he pictures himself in the pits at the Indianapolis Motor Speedway, waiting to jump on the next blowout. "Four minutes" he declares confidently to the family when a tire blows on the trip home from Christmas-tree shopping.

His replacement tire in the trunk is qualitatively akin to the bargain-basement furnace coal that causes his clinkers. Shep says the Old Man's spare "tires were actually only tires in the academic sense. They were round, they had once been made of rubber." Quite a contrast to the tires used at Indy. And even with Ralphie's help changing the tire, complicated by the Old Man's impatience that led him to knock over the hub cap containing the wheel hardware, it takes him eight minutes to replace the tire—hardly a Hohman Speedway record. Oh well, try again next time, mister master mechanic. Technological hope springs eternal.

## Do Real Men Need Help?

As I suggest throughout the book, Shepherd had a fairly dim view of men—himself included. In the movie, he wants to convey the idea that men, like women, can't do everything themselves. They need help. The problem is that men wrongly tend to assume that they don't need advice, counsel, and even basic instructions. They see themselves as freestanding experts on whatever problem they are facing, from travel directions to auto repair.

The Old Man is also challenged by the Parker abode's electrical system. He's clever at loading up electrical outlets with dozens of extension cords, adapters, and plugs. But sparks fly whenever he has to tangle with wires in order to plug in new devices such as the leg lamp and the Christmas tree. Shep says of the Old Man's household electrical expertise, "[He] could replace fuses quicker than a jackrabbit on a date. He bought them by the gross." That's one way to tackle overloaded circuits.

One of the reasons the Old Man has difficulty tackling technology is that he doesn't listen to counsel—even to obvious truth from a trustworthy source. In Shepherd's view, this is a deeply male issue: Men assume that they can successfully solve any technological problem, as if they always have enough common sense and necessary expertise. The Old Man confuses a blue Christmas tree bulb for a green one. He and Mom trade barbs about which of them is "color-blind"—a kind way for her to remind her overconfident husband that he's wrong, again.

I love the Old Man's line about Ralphie getting him a new furnace for Christmas. For just a moment, we see that the Old Man knows he's technologically underwater. He might be the head of the household, but he's no match for all of the slings and arrows of gadgets and doo-dads that will come his way. A brand-new furnace might help, tempo-rarily. Fewer clinkers, perhaps, particularly if he upgrades the quality of the coal that he shovels into his basement beast. But novel technologies invariably create new snafus. He can either call in the technological gurus to do their magic, or keep scuffling in the ashen battlefield of semi-incompetence.

One more extension cord is not adequate for tackling a household electrical system. But I can say, as a male, that I feel better when the technology completely malfunctions because then I can overcome my ego by calling in the priestly pros to tackle the problem. Or, better yet, I can buy a fancy new device that promises true heavenly experiences. Just don't try to sell me any stinkin' warranty plan; that's kid's stuff for low-tech altar boys, not a manly choice for a high-tech prelate like me.

## CHAPTER 8

# Don't Trust the Media

In his collection of stories, *A Fistful of Fig Newtons*, Jean Shepherd used a thematic word that encapsulates his view of the media: *mendacity*, meaning a lie or falsehood. He believed that we should not automatically trust the media because they are often deceitful. From his perspective, many popular media feed us fabricated views of reality, tale by tale, in both news and entertainment. We're all swimming in a sea of mediated information, disinformation, and misinformation. It's not always possible to tell the difference. *Caveat emptor*—buyer beware!

Shepherd's life lesson about not mindlessly trusting the media also runs through *A Christmas Story*. It starts early, when Ralphie is captivated by a Red Ryder BB rifle ad he sees in *Boys' Life* magazine, and which is affirmed in a Higbee's department store window display. He inserts the full-page ad in his mother's bedside copy of *Look* magazine, hoping to catch her eye and convince her to get him the rifle for Christmas.

## How Did the Old Man Know What Ralphie Wanted for Christmas?

After inserting the Red Ryder rifle ad in Mom's *Look* magazine, Ralphie actually places the magazine on his father's bed. Is that how the Old Man determines what Ralphie desperately wants for Christmas? Or does the Old Man "just know," through father-son "osmosis," like a genetic connection with primordial origins? As the Old Man says while Ralphie unwraps the rifle on Christmas, "I had one when I was eight years old." Like father, like son, from generation to generation. Related question: Does the Old Man need to give Ralphie the rifle more than Ralphie needs to receive it?

Ralphie believes the ad's claim that the BB rifle will make him a family-protecting neighborhood sharpshooter—or, at least, he wants to believe that dreamy hype. The wildly popular Red Ryder hero, portrayed in actual movies and comic books, affirms Ralphie's hopes.

Shepherd told me that nearly everyone thinks they are immune to the effects of the media. In truth, he claimed, most of us are suckers. If media content confirms what we already believe—or want to believe—we don't seriously question it. So, the media feed us our own propaganda. In effect, we and the media together propagandize ourselves.

To Shepherd, this reflects a sick media system. Media professionals generally pander to audiences and then take their resulting paychecks home. Why risk telling the truth, losing audiences, and getting fired? Strongly put, that's Shepherd's premise about the state of media in modern America, going back at least to the post–World War II era—and increasingly worse since then. That's why he used the word "mendacity" in *A Fistful of Fig Newtons*—to capture our deceptive media environment.

The Old Man's "major award," a leg lamp, results from his brilliant contest submission to a newspaper. For me, one of the drollest—and truest—scenes in the movie occurs when the Old Man tells Mom that he's determined to win the fifty-thousand-dollar (the equivalent of over a million dollars today) first prize by matching wits with other contestants in a battle over who knows more about "Great Characters in American Literature."

He's stumped, but Mom instantly gives him the answer to the history-making fact: The name of the Lone Ranger's nephew's horse is Victor. "Everyone knows that," Mom tells him, but he apparently doesn't hear—or want to hear—her chiding him. He wants to believe that he can do the puzzle on his own, without assistance from others. Why admit his lack of knowledge? Why question the silliness of the question, especially because he now has the answer?

Moreover, why does the Old Man think that Victor is a great literary figure? Does he even ask the question, providing a modicum of media discernment? Why does he suppose that the contest is anything more than a raffle of thousands of correctly completed puzzles? He's being played, not just playing the game—and willingly so.

Then the Old Man cites a newspaper article about a guy who allegedly swallowed a yo-yo on a bet. The victim must have had a gigantic larynx or a teensy yo-yo. "The poor guy," says the Old Man, looking down his nose at those who aren't as brilliant as him, was "some clodhopper down in Griffith, Indiana." The Old Man brilliantly determines that he's above the level of a pitiable clodhopper (a dull, stupid person) from downstate, presumably where all of the idiots dwell.

Mom, the reasonable skeptic, replies, "Boy, they write the silliest things in the newspaper." But the Old Man doesn't buy her logic. He says the yo-yo tale is "real news," not like that "politics slop." So much for the Old Man's incisive media discernment: Political news coverage is "slop." There's probably some truth to that. Clearly, he's no fan of politicians, anyway. But is swallowing a yo-yo real news? I guess it would be if it actually occurred. The headline sure would attract my attention, even though it sounds like bait. When it comes to critiquing news, the Old Man appears to be an upstate clodhopper.

## Do We All Consume Media That Confirm Our Biases?

Shepherd believed that we all want to believe the media whose messages we already agree with—or want to agree with. Media scholars call it "confirmation bias." Mom gives the Old Man a chance to reconsider some of his media biases, but he won't budge. He's made up his mind about what's straightforward or disingenuous, serious or silly, news or entertainment. To Shepherd, the Old Man thereby symbolizes the plight of all people in a media-saturated world. We don't have the time, energy, or willpower to seek out media that challenge what we already believe.

In Shepherd's view, consumers naïvely pass along stories they see, hear, or read in media, thereby expanding the impact of media on society. Consumers also relay what someone else tells them that they saw, read, or heard. The ever-more-exaggerated or even revised versions of media tales give us all something to talk about as self-congratulatory citizens: "Did you know . . . ?" "I heard that . . ." Newsy gossip abounds among us all, especially regarding politics and the weather. Just don't try to pass along questionable sports news to a real sports junkie; they are textual literalists who enjoy correcting ill-informed fans like me. Shepherd nailed me on a couple of my erroneous football stats.

As Shepherd saw it, entertainment yarns, news blurbs, urban legends, and juicy gossip all intermingle and then circulate quicker than anyone can master. He said that fish don't know that they live in water, no matter how polluted the lake. We humans aren't fully aware that we dwell in a soup-like media world composed of bits of information and disinformation as well as a few indistinguishable facts and truths, here and there. We slurp down the slop, in tune with our preexisting assumptions. Fish take in toxic water from sewers and steel plants, unaware of better water in cleaner ponds. For them, everything is dandy. For us, self-confirming media toxicity seems just as normal as fish's contaminated water. Who needs alternative news when the existing narratives sound about right?

Did Schwartz's old man actually see a guy at work stick his tongue to a frozen railroad track? Even if so, did it really take the fire department to remove his tongue from the steel?

Did Ralphie's Old Man know for certain that a fellow in Terre Haute won a bowling alley in a newspaper contest? What a terrific gift! Imagine suddenly inheriting a bowling alley in a downstate town. You pack up your kinfolk and move there, like Jed and his family on *The Beverly Hillbillies*, only to discover it's a barely functioning business mired in cigarette butts and foul beer smells, not to mention the mold and mildew, along with the buckets collecting the water leaking through the patched-up roof. Now, that's quite a "major" award. It would be like winning a used car in a contest; then it turns out, the auto was last seen floating down the Mississippi River during a flood, with two cormorants resting proudly on the hood, heads turned upward like the Chinese-restaurant duck.

## Are All Media Becoming "Tabloids"?

Shepherd felt that sensationalism was becoming the primary means for all media to attract audiences. To him, the supermarket tabloids were the cutting edge of modern "journalism," leading the way for tabloid-like TV shows masquerading as news. I can only imagine what he would have thought about today's social media as purveyors of sensationalism.

I was in a supermarket checkout lane, clandestinely peeking at the front pages of the colorful tabloids. I spotted the *National Enquirer*, a high-circulation, first-rate news source if ever there was one. On the cover was a photo of a popular TV evangelist departing a cheap motel room with an alleged prostitute—his shiny new Lincoln Continental parked in the weedy lot. Great! I was writing a book on TV evangelists. I sneaked the paper under my groceries on the conveyer belt.

Sitting in my car in the store lot, I fumbled through the tabloid because they don't include a table of contents to help you quickly check out the stories at the cash register. Amazing! Then I had a close encounter with slipshod reporting: I was quoted in the article! Me—including my university credentials. What? It sounded like something I would have said, but the *Enquirer* never interviewed me. Still, I could now tell friends and family that I was quoted in a national "paper" with a total audience reach of 5.3 million people. I was famous. An authority. Maybe I could get a CNN contract as a special correspondent covering the seamy side of down-home religion. Sins sell—especially sex-related sins, the juicier the more enticing.

According to Shepherd, the popular entertainment complex is not entirely trustworthy. The *Little Orphan Annie* radio show scene in *A Christmas Story* is simultaneously funny and tragic. Ralphie consumes

gallons of Ovaltine chocolate drink to get
enough coupons to send in for his special
decoder ring; Ovaltine was the show's
sponsor. Then he waits forever to receive
the ring in the mail, checking the mail-
box daily, earnestly listening nightly to
the program. According to Shep, the
popular broadcast is the only thing that
could drag Ralphie away from the new leg lamp's "soft glow of sex."
Seduction takes many forms.

When the decoder ring arrives, the package includes a special cer-
tificate of membership. "Master Ralph Parker" is proudly "appointed
a member of the Little Orphan Annie secret circle, and is entitled to
all of the honors and benefits accruing thereto." Shep reports that it
was signed personally by Little Orphan Annie and countersigned by
program host Pierre Andre, who had one of the smoothest, most trustworthy voices in radio. Already at the age of nine, Ralphie becomes a
member of an identity group of sorts, a true "master."

When Ralphie decodes his first message, however, he's in for a
sobering shocker about media mendacity. It reads, "Be sure to drink
your Ovaltine." The top-secret message,
supposedly from Annie herself, is just a
"crummy commercial," mutters Ralphie.
Incensed, Ralphie whispers the SOB
term to himself. He has met the media-
entertainment complex face-to-face. He
will never again admire the famed Annie
and Pierre. Shep says that Ralphie "went
out to face the world again. Wiser."

Ironically, only seconds earlier, in Ralphie's naïveté, the "whole
fate of the planet" was hanging in the balance as he decoded that

first message. He goes from being proudly inducted into a prestigious secret society to whispering an expletive. Talk about rapid media disillusionment!

## Was the Red Ryder Rifle Real?

Shepherd was absolutely convinced that the Daisy company manufactured a "Red Ryder carbine-action, 200-shot range model air rifle with a compass in the stock and this thing that tells time." But no such rifle existed in 1940. Chances are that Shepherd recalled a combination of rifle features from different manufacturers during his childhood, likely promoted by ads in magazines he read. He had convinced himself of something that was not true.

Shepherd said that Santa, in the movie, is like a cultural god, omnipresent and omnipotent—the go-to source to have holiday prayers come true—or so believed young Ralphie and his hopeful buddies.

This is why Shepherd plays up the fake Santa at Higbee's. The rather unsaintly Santa and his nasty minions are just trying to make an hourly wage. Santa says to the elf who commands the slide: "If Higbee thinks I'm working one minute past nine, he can kiss my foot" (the same smelly, black-booted foot that will push Ralphie down the slide). The dual elves, who are working with the red-nosed Santa, process the kids like a factory production line. They holler at children to quickly deliver their pleas to Santa. Then they discard the kids by tossing them down the exit slide. Ho, ho, ho!

While sitting on Santa's lap, Ralphie gets spooked and temporarily forgets the gift that he absolutely must receive on the big day. Dearly beloved Santa goads him into saying "football." For a second, it looks like Ralphie will have a chance—as he hangs on to the exit slide, just below Santa—to change his plea deal. But Santa delivers that echoed phrase, "You'll shoot your eye out, kid," and shoves Ralphie down the slide with his shiny boot, accompanied with the customary, "Ho, ho, ho!" Clearly, Santa is no saint.

During the movie, we repeatedly see the Old Man reading newspaper comics and sports pages. He lives in his own mediated world of fun, fantasy, and fake news, while Mom goes to sleep dreaming about the images in *Look* magazine and Ralphie chases his dreams in *Boys' Life*.

In an earlier version of the script, Mom's bedtime reading of choice was *Modern Romances*, but that magazine was designed to appeal to younger, mostly single women. Also, the magazine signified that Mom was not entirely happy with being married to the Old Man, who may have lacked some romantic sensitivities toward her. But the switch to *Look* magazine worked for Shepherd, who disliked *Look* magazine because, in his view, it offered vicarious "pictures" of the world rather than a rational analysis of the days' public affairs. To him, many Americans tend to "look at" rather than understand the world.

Shepherd's life lesson about distrusting media is based partly on his experiences in the entertainment business. He told me he knew celebrities who pretended to be virtuous people, but were often phonies who disdained their fans. Shepherd said that most Hollywood stars don't even watch their own movies or TV shows because they can't stand the productions. He claimed that the "biz" is all about money and social status. He remained cynical about the very industry in which he made a living. Yet, he always found worthy exceptions, never giving up all hope for media redemption.

Today, the media are even more intrusive and omnipotent than in the era depicted in the film. Families rarely watch and discuss television together—let alone listen to the radio together. Everyone has his or her own "electronic device" to consume media like popping candy. Millions are essentially addicted to social media and devoted to cell phones. Writer Stephen King refers to the mobile phone as a "slave bracelet."

The ads and celebrity promos show up everywhere around us. Younger adults get most of their news from social media. It's difficult to navigate this kind of media world without being suckered into believing that the media we ourselves consume are also the most honest and accurate purveyors of truth, and that media celebrities are actually like the images depicted in the media by their publicists. Whom can we trust in a world of media mendacity?

The media change over time, but distrusting the media remains a worthy life lesson. Maybe we should follow the kind of dictum offered by President Ronald Reagan about international treaties: "Trust, but verify." Ironically, the media don't tell us, but that expression is actually a Russian proverb.

According to Shepherd, as foretold in *A Christmas Story*, there might be a finer line between the *National Enquirer*, the *New York Times*, CNN, and even Santa than we are inclined to acknowledge. Maybe the supermarket tabloids indeed represented the cutting edge of our so-called media "revolution," providing role models for the social media. Ho, ho, ho!

## CHAPTER 9

# Be a Good Neighbor

Neighbors. We've all had terrific and questionable ones. Some of the worst feuds are fought across backyard fences. Some of the kindest gestures occur neighbor to neighbor in times of need.

Then there are the Bumpuses, with over seven hundred hound dogs scrounging around the vicinity. I wonder what the entire Bumpus house and yard looked like. Jean Shepherd and I talked a lot about the Bumpuses, who make up an escapade in one of his books.

A bumpkin is someone who's culturally inexperienced, lacks social grace, and is probably from the country rather than an urban area with art galleries, gourmet restaurants, and parks for well-dressed walkers with silk clothing and glittering jewelry. Acclaimed artist Georges Seurat didn't paint bumpkins in his French parks.

## Where Did Shepherd Find the Name "Bumpus"?

Shepherd said that he wanted a bumpkin-designating name for the "uncultured" neighbors in his stories. He took the last name of "Bumpus" from some actual neighbors back in Indiana. Ironically—once again—the real Bumpus family was not made up of hillbillies. In fact, it was quite a respected family. The particular Bumpus kid that Shepherd actually went to school with became a decorated war veteran.

But it's not just a high-class versus low-class issue related to social status or culture. There is much more to the unseen Bumpus characters and their unrestrained hounds, forever plaguing the Old Man.

Shepherd said that the Bumpuses represent the fear we all have that uncivilized people will move in nearby, take over the neighborhood, and eventually destroy civilization across entire cities or countries.

Of course, not everyone will agree on what is or is not civilized. Parking on the lawn in most Florida neighborhoods is far more acceptable than doing so here in West Michigan. When I was living in Florida, the city council tried to pass a municipal code that would ban parking on home lawns. Citizens were up in arms—some of them literally—and the council chickened out, even though you could still have chickens in cages in your backyard. My guess is that if the lawn-parking ban had been up for a vote, it would have lost by over 80 percent. Many neighbors were outraged at the attempt to curtail their "civil liberties."

During that lawn-parking brouhaha, my wife and I wrote a Florida Christmas song to the tune of "Chestnuts roasting on an open fire . . ." It began, "Pickups rusting on Augustine grass . . ."

Shepherd himself moved from the east to the west side of Florida partly out of fear of what he perceived was occurring on city streets in the Miami area. Drug deals. Fights. Shootings. Gangs. Road rage. Like a lot of people today, Shepherd in the 1980s was already worried about the future of civil society.

Shepherd strongly supported law-enforcement professionals. But he believed that they couldn't completely curtail gross misbehavior. In other words, incivility is not just a governmental issue. It's also personal, related to family upbringing, neighborhood life, and personal conscience.

His solution is a life lesson in *A Christmas Story*: Be a good neighbor. No one is exempt. Those who refuse to act like decent neighbors are either nincompoops or malcontents—or both. Of course, sometimes we ourselves are the scalawags, perhaps unintentionally.

The bumpkin-like Bumpus clan represents the growing lack of good neighbors in society. Their hounds are a wonderful cinematic device. The dogs convey the apparent coarseness of the neighbors without having to depict the actual Bumpus family. After all, how do you portray uncivil people without relying on a stereotype that would likely cast aspersions on everyone seemingly represented by the group?

Shepherd's warning is that anyone can become an unneighborly Bumpus, although some people seem to be more prone to being such culprits. There is hillbilly in all of us.

The Bumpus beasts seemed to be everywhere, day and night, roaming around while wheezing, sniffing, howling, and snarfing up whatever they could find that smelled vaguely like garbage. Shepherd said to me, elaborating on the story, that the dogs survived partly on the food scraps tossed off the back porch of the Bumpuses' ramshackle house, under which the beasts cohabitated and copulated, producing increasingly demented beasts through inbreeding.

In other words, the Bumpuses are not decent enough neighbors to train and control their dogs. The Bumpuses themselves might be pleasant and even friendly people. But for some reason they lack such neighborliness.

## How Many Hounds Do the Bumpuses Own?

All we know for sure in the movie, according to Shep, is that the neighbors are "hillbillies" who own 785 hounds. Of course, the actual number of dogs used in shooting was much fewer—only four of them. And that handful of canine "actors" was not always willing to perform. Being well fed, they weren't even interested in attacking the turkey, so the pooch owner didn't feed them the day before the turkey scene.

By using the term "hillbilly," itself a stereotype, Shepherd was trying to capture the idea of people who live in vast open areas and don't have to abide by the social etiquette of city dwellers. They are "hill folk," to use another term popular after the Great Depression, when southern, hill-dwelling people started moving north.

"Hillbilly" is not a perfect, stereotype-free label, but Shepherd figured that by not depicting the actual Bumpuses he would be using it in the least stereotypical way. He said he just couldn't find anything better, which most people could not tie to a particular group that they come into contact with occasionally. In other words, for most Americans, the hillbillies are "out there," like a kind of scary, imaginary group (as well as somewhat inside each of us). Hillbillies exist as myth. As far as I know, few people self-identify as hillbillies and there is no representative group lobbying the U.S. Congress for hillbilly rights.

---

## Why Did the Bumpus Hounds Like the Old Man?

It's easy to fall into the trap of thinking that the Bumpus hounds disliked the Old Man. They were always bothering him. Weren't they? But Shep says, ironically, that the smelly dogs "ignored every other human being on earth but my Old Man." These beasts had a thing for him. Perhaps they enjoyed giving him grief even though they apparently didn't feel like hassling anyone else. Was the Old Man a "victim" of friendly pooches? Perhaps the Old Man smelled like a canine delicacy because of the buckets of red cabbage he ingested. Perhaps it was his Olds' rumble; dogs do tend to gravitate toward particular vehicles that seem to broadcast just the right racket. Here's the irony, from Shepherd: The Old Man himself was something of a Bumpus! Growling Bumpuses attract, and even like, other growling Bumpuses! Woof, woof!

---

To complicate matters, one neighbor's delight can be another neighbor's nuisance. My wife and I rented a home in Florida where the family across the street seemingly lived in their open, two-stall garage—furniture, refrigerator, and all. They liked to barbeque there and play loud music from a boom box, speakers facing toward the street. Actually, we liked the music, but not after ten at night.

I asked them to turn down the volume a bit, and they were happy to do so. They seemed like entirely decent people whom I would enjoy getting to know if we lived there permanently. I bet they wondered why anyone in their right mind would go to sleep so early. They probably shook their heads at us, the goofy renters. This was a very pleasant neighborhood with higher-end homes. We were the interlopers.

Any of us can slip into becoming bad neighbors. One wrong act can lead to a similarly bad response. The next thing we know, we are dwelling with the Hatfields or McCoys, feuding for generations.

In *A Christmas Story*, the setup for the Christmas-morning turkey disaster is based partly on the Old Man's insatiable appetite for the roasted bird. Shep says that the Old Man was truly a "turkey junkie." This is not the family's everyday meat loaf, but a special cuisine reserved for a holiday. To the Old Man, roast turkey was far more civilized and socially upscale than the grub likely snarfed down by the Bumpuses.

So, when the dogs invade the Parker kitchen, it's not just a matter of mangy mutts going after the beautifully cooked bird. It's seen by the Old Man as a major breach of social etiquette. In his view, a callous cluster of bumpkins is attacking the relatively more civilized, comparatively upscale world of the hardworking, respectable Old Man and his civil kin.

Doesn't this type of social dynamic affect all of us? We look up and down our neighborhood streets and make judgments about people's social and cultural standings. What is the condition of their lawns?

Which houses in our neighborhood are freshly painted in the latest colors? What about nicely trimmed bushes and ornamental trees with special-colored mulch accenting them aesthetically? Who doesn't complain to family about some neighbors' outrageous statuary or ugly lawn ornaments? We all size up one another's appearances and manners in different situations. We scout for signs of Bumpuses invading the neighborhood. After all, neighbors who don't control their mutts might be an omen of far worse things to come.

I'm still amazed that my HOA lets me display our full-size, illuminated leg lamp every Christmas season. "For sale" signs are officially forbidden—and you never see them except for an open house. My questionably erotic and well-lit statuary is not outlawed? Perhaps humor, associated with the lamp and the movie in my case, creates a more relaxed sense of neighborliness.

## Was Shepherd Himself a Bit of a Bumpus?

When you move into a Home Owner's Association (HOA), personal differences in cultural and artistic taste can become matters of legalistic dispute. In fact, Shepherd himself caused grief for his HOA on Sanibel Island, Florida. His ham radio antenna was not permitted, but he refused to take it down. In that sense, maybe he was a bit of a Bumpus.

One of the dirty little secrets about HOA rules and regulations is that enforcement often depends on the cultural tastes of the board members. One board's notion of a restricted backyard tree house suddenly becomes an acceptable playhouse to a different board member with children.

When the Old Man comes home to giddily announce he's won a major award, he temporarily becomes a more charitable neighbor, even to the Bumpuses. He sticks his foot out the back door to let the hounds take a nibble and says, "Come on, have a chew, fellas, on me. It's my gift." Is he that happy about the prize? Or does he secretly like the attention he receives from the hounds? Don't we all dream about being socially uncouth at times?

As the Old Man slams the door closed, however, an ear of one of the hounds gets stuck in it. The Old Man has to reopen the door to release the beast. In spite of his temporary generosity, the Old Man took great delight in catching the beast's appendage in the door: "Serves ya right ya smelly buggers!" Yet he's the one who opened the door in the first place!

But when the Bumpuses' mongrels abscond with the Parkers' beautiful turkey, the battle of neighbor versus neighbor is back in operation. The Old Man loses his cool. Emotionally beside himself, stammering for just the right words, he says, "Go on home, you mangy mutts. Get out of here, you rotten, filthy . . . Hey, Bumpus. Get over here and get your stinking dogs." It's the only time in the movie he directly addresses the invisible Bumpuses. The Old Man is left defeated on the battleground. All he has left to fight with are words, which the Bumpuses themselves might not even hear. So funny! And so tragic.

Yet, irony nearly always sneaks up on us in Shepherd's life lessons. What's good for our goose (or duck, or turkey) is good for the gander (the other neighbors).

Earlier in the movie, the Old Man, thinking he's more socially advanced than the rubes next door, gets smitten by the perceived beauty of his major award. He bigheadedly places the glowing leg "sculpture" in the front window for all of Cleveland Street to enjoy. Clouded by pride in his victory, he can't perceive the potentially offensive message he's flashing down the road. Would a civilized person do this? Or is civilization declining in his own domicile?

Mom tries to be more neighborly by turning off the lamp a few times, and then shutting it down for good by breaking it. Perhaps the leg lamp is a more refined neighborly option than the Bumpuses' noisy, flatulent dogs. But what makes the Old Man such a model neighbor?

The Old Man might never be able to achieve peace with the Bumpus hounds because the mutts either love or hate him so much. But maybe he could have accepted his wife's offer to talk with him about not placing the lighted leg lamp squarely in the front window every night. One neighbor's smelly hound dog is another one's tawdry window lamp. What's your hillbilly secret?

## 10

# Admit When You Do Wrong

An important life lesson in *A Christmas Story* is admitting when we do wrong. Jean Shepherd told me that we humans are not inclined to fess up when we do things that might emotionally hurt or physically harm others. In the back of our minds, we tend to think that someone else has "caused" our transgression. We hope to pass the blame, not accept it.

Sometimes guilt drives us to reveal our transgressions, but often we think we can get away without punishment—by people or God. Our consciences are similarly inadequate to control our behaviors. As a result, we keep quiet, pretending that *we* are the righteous folks and *others* deserve the blame.

And this is true for all of us, said Shepherd. No matter how righteous, privileged, or moral we think we are, we sometimes fail to come forward when we should.

In *A Christmas Story*, Schwartz and Ralphie know that they shouldn't leave Flick in the schoolyard alone, his tongue stuck to the flagpole. Schwartz himself had dared Flick to place his tongue there. Ralphie witnesses the fiasco firsthand, letting it proceed according to the rules of daring one another. They are complicit in Flick's awful plight, but they abandon their buddy anyway. They dash back into the school building when the bell rings, leaving Flick to a potentially calamitous destiny. In fact, no students report the catastrophe to Miss Shields or presumably any other teacher or administrator. Silence. Amazing!

Remember that in the few seconds before the bell rings, Flick offers desperate pleas, muffled because of his inoperable tongue: "Don't leave, come back. Come back. Don't leave me. Come back." It reminds me of poor Randy rolling back and forth on the snowy ground and desperately calling for help. Flick is almost crying, truly scared. Apparently, this is an entirely new experience for everyone on the playground—a novel episode in the history of Warren G. Harding School. Flick is being abandoned by his alleged pals. We know that they should tell Miss Shields that he's out there all alone, flapping his arms like broken wings while his tongue is bonded to the pole.

In the classroom, Schwartz and Ralphie play dumb when Miss Shields asks about the absent Flick: "Has anyone seen Flick? He was at recess, wasn't he?" As viewers, we wonder what's happening with Flick in the schoolyard. Is he still anchored to the pole, calling miserably for help? Maybe he will just rip his tongue off the pole and end up in the hospital? Who knows? This is new terrain for everyone.

## Why Does Shepherd Use Biblical Analogies in *A Christmas Story*?

As a teller of parables about the human condition, Shepherd regularly used biblical analogies. For instance, Shep explains how Schwartz and Ralphie are dealing psychologically with Miss Shields' inquisition: "Flick? Flick who?" Feigned ignorance! It's the great human response to guilt, played out in the biblical book of Genesis after Adam and Eve eat the forbidden fruit. Pretend you weren't involved. Hide. Above all, don't stare face-to-face with your examiner (Miss Shields), who might be able to read your expression and peg your guilt. Far more than I am able to describe in this book, Shepherd, raised a nominal Presbyterian, uses basic biblical analogies to underscore the deeper aspects of the drama of everyday life.

Miss Shields personalizes her query—like God suddenly asking Adam directly what occurred in the garden of Eden: "Ralphie, do you know where Flick is?" Ralphie offers an unconvincing look of innocence. Miss Shields can see right through it, but what can *she* do? She's a judge without evidence. Everyone is innocent until proven guilty!

Miss Shields is frustrated but wise. She appeals to all of the students' senses of guilt, assuming that there is at least a tinge of remorse somewhere in the class, and hoping that someone will come forward with the facts of the case. She says, sternly, "I said, has anyone seen Flick?"

It appears that all students are going to play dumb, even though some of them were at the scene of the crime.

Shepherd believed that each of us who has done something wrong has imagined being questioned like this. We replay the scenario in our minds. What will we say? How can we be somewhat truthful without exactly admitting our own role? We go through life accumulating lower-level guilt. We roll our snowball of guilt through new fields of fresh snowfall, as if preparing to make a snowman—a statue or idol of our private guilt. Fortunately, the guilt-accumulating snowballs eventually melt; we guilty people forget about the transgressions and learn to live with ourselves once again. Until we have to avoid accepting responsibility the next time.

Finally, the truth emerges in the classroom about Flick's whereabouts—thanks to classmate Esther Jane, who secretly points toward the classroom window. Miss Shields glances out the window to the playground, spots Flick, and offers a classic biblical response: "Oh, my G-d." This is serious. She runs to the scene, without a coat or hat. She must be motherly to Flick, comforting him through the double trauma of injuring his tongue and being abandoned by friends.

The fire department and the cops arrive. The classmates run to the window to watch the saga unfold. Schwartz's daring of Flick to put his tongue on the icy pole has produced a bona fide human debacle. Miss Shields comforts poor Flick. What else can she do at this point? The double and triple dares have been effectively executed, although she's unaware. Flick's tongue is released from the pole—though it's not clear exactly how.

Back in the classroom, Miss Shields deepens her inquisition. She's peeved—probably more than she appears to be. And she suspects who the guilty parties are—one or both of Flick's two closest pals. Miss Shields says, "Now I know that some of you put Flick up to this.

But he has refused to say who." Wow, Flick loyally protects the guilty Schwartz! She continues, "But those who did it know their blame. And I'm sure that the guilt you feel is far worse than any punishment you might receive." She said, "*Those* who did it." Hmm. Does she know the two leading culprits? Or is she suggesting collective guilt for everyone who watched it happen?

## How Do They Remove Flick's Tongue from the Flagpole?

My friends who are emergency workers tell me that you merely have to pour warm water on the frozen metal to "unstick" a tongue; no big deal. But in the film, the director wants to have Flick reenter the classroom dramatically with a bandaged tongue, so it appears like Flick's tongue might have been ripped off the pole. Ouch! Nothing like leaving your taste buds on an ice-cold piece of steel. In the shooting, Flick's tongue was actually held to the plastic pole at a hole that provided suction from an invisible vacuum pump.

Shep tells us what Schwartz and Ralphie and the other students are really thinking: "Adults love to say things like that, but kids know better. We knew darn well it was always better not to get caught."

Nevertheless, Miss Shields is on a roll! Preach it, woman! She says calmly but firmly, "Now, don't you feel terrible? Don't you feel remorse for what you have done?"

When Miss Shields questions the class about Flick's run-in with the flagpole, Ralphie and Schwartz both look around the room like they are saying, nonverbally, "Who, me? Can't be me. I'm innocent."

Miss Shields can probably tell from the way the two transgressors are avoiding eye contact with her that they are the rascals. In fact, she first questions Ralphie directly, asking if he knows where Flick is. Alas, no proof! The court must be adjourned.

An interesting aspect of *A Christmas Story* is that the Old Man is pretty consistently wrong about things—or at least misguided—but he never directly apologizes. Even Mom's loving correction will not get him to budge from his self-righteousness.

For instance, he insists that he has correctly identified the color of the broken Christmas tree light, but he's wrong and Mom is correct. He similarly messes up on straightening the star on the tree—actually making the entire top of the tree worse and nearly falling off the ladder to boot. Yet Mom tells him the star is fine before he risks a broken hip.

In the case of blurting out the "F" word while changing the tire with the Old Man, Ralphie is in a real pickle. He can't deny what he's said. And the Old Man tells Mom what Ralphie uttered, perhaps partly to shift the focus from the fact that he was woefully slow in his race to replace the tire in four minutes "flat."

Instead of protesting or complaining that he needs justice as a victim in the family mess, Ralphie simply makes the best of the situation. But why wouldn't the Old Man admit that he might be the primary source of Ralphie learning the "F" word in the first place? How in the world could his knowledge of his own swearing get so far out of sync with reality? Still, Ralphie is stuck. He can either blame the Old Man or pass the buck to someone else, like an innocent buddy.

Shep describes how the fearful Ralphie initially felt after uttering the forbidden F-word: "I was dead. What would it be? The guillotine? Hanging? The chair? The rack? The Chinese water torture? Mere child's play compared to what surely awaited me." Ralphie knows that he's in deep trouble even though he was just mouthing the same "queen of dirty words" that the Old Man offered up in earshot of Ralphie "at least ten times a day."

Ralphie buckles, falsely blaming Schwartz for the source of his F-bomb. Then Ralphie witnesses Mom calling Schwartz's mother to transmit blame to a guiltless friend. Shep calls it "another shot of mysterious, inexorable, official justice." Well, it's certainly not blind justice, even if the Old Man is somewhat blind to his spicy vocabulary.

Ralphie is prepared to accept correction from Mom—verbally and with soap sucking—but not to fess up to the bigger truth of the Old Man's involvement. Just as Flick protected Schwartz at school, Ralphie protects his father. The Old Man will go scot-free, like Ralphie and Schwartz did in the classroom after Flick's daring submission to the triple-dog-dare, tongue-to-metal challenge at the flagpole.

Ralphie moves beyond the immediate situation by doing his mouth-cleaning penitence. He semicontritely sucks on a bar of red Lifebuoy soap, supposedly letting it purify his soul from the depth of his guilt—like bathroom purgatory.

## Why Lifebuoy Soap?

Over time, Ralphie had become quite a connoisseur of soap, says Shep: "My personal preference is for Lux, but I found Palmolive had a nice, piquant, after-dinner flavor. Heady, but with just a touch of mellow smoothness. Lifebuoy, on the other hand . . ." Sounds like an afficionado describing fine wine. But Shepherd also loved the name "Lifebuoy" as a kind of moral navigation mark (buoy) for the life of a boy. Sucking on that soap is a sign you are headed in the wrong direction in life; you might even be lost at sea. The actual red bar used in the movie was made of wax.

Actually, Ralphie winks at the camera, knowing that the punishment is pretty thin and that he avoided the brunt of it by passing the blame to Schwartz. Oh, such justice! If only Adam and Eve could have just blamed the serpent, sucked on Lifebuoy, and winked at each other. It would have changed the course of biblical history.

Shepherd embellishes all kids' natural sense of injustice, however, with the dream scene of Ralphie returning home as a blind adult. Ralphie aims to lay a guilt trip on Mom and the Old Man for their years of allegedly unjust punishments. "What brought you to this lowly state?" asks the Old Man, in tears along with Mom. Mom asks, "What did we do? Oh please, Ralph [he's no longer just "Ralphie" and has the upper hand]. I must know what we did." Ralphie tells them, "Soap poisoning. . . . I'll manage to get along somehow." Mom, the more-sensitive parent, replies, "I'll never forgive myself." That's what Ralphie wants to hear. Genuine remorse! And tangible justice!? Maybe—but probably only in Ralphie's dreams.

Yet Mom is really a softy, hardly meriting such treatment by her son. Mom's post–soap punishment for Ralphie is merely requiring that Ralphie not turn on any lights in the bedroom that night and refrain from reading comic books—as if he could see them in the dark anyway.

Shepherd always told me that life is too messy to "fix" everything. He also said that women are more likely than men to admit when they are wrong. We need to be understanding and to care for each other in the midst of the "slop" of injustice.

Mom does a pretty good job of this. She's smart; she knows when the men in her family are just posturing. But she doesn't want to rock the boat and create greater disharmony. After all, in Shepherd's view, women normally have to do the "cleanup" when domestic matters go awry.

We all foul up sometimes and then have to live with the consequences of our improper words and deeds. But actual justice doesn't always come easy. We eternally hide, posture, and pass the guilt. Sometimes we even feel good when we get away with a misdeed—like Schwartz and Ralphie successfully avoiding the blame from Miss Shields for Flick's flagpole incident. Still, admitting when we are wrong is a great life lesson that can help us avoid short-term conflicts and longer-term guilt. We might even stop winking at ourselves in the mirror when we wrongly get off the hook.

# CHAPTER 11

## Play Fair

Jean Shepherd loved fair competition, especially in sports. Watching a well-played college or professional football game with him was a joy. He appreciated great plays and fine performances. When his hometown Chicago Bears were playing great football during the mid-1980s, he was on cloud nine.

At the same time, Shepherd believed that we humans don't always play fair in the game of life. We dishonorably take advantage of one another, bending the rules of proper social interactions.

One of Shepherd's life lessons in *A Christmas Story* is that we should play fair. Otherwise, we shouldn't expect others to treat us fairly.

Fairness starts with us as individuals and families, and then impacts our neighborhood, society, business, government, and beyond.

For Shepherd, fair play is a moral code intrinsic to humankind. He couldn't imagine a society where fair play was not the standard for life. Like many of us, he held high standards for others, but sometimes fell short of his own expectations for himself.

I watch the annual TV-news reports of shoppers charging into stores at the opening bell on Black Friday, the day after Thanksgiving, to get their mitts on sale items before others can. Every year, fights break out. Amazing. If stores hired referees, many shoppers would receive fouls. The battles represent the dark side of human nature. The season of giving becomes a time of grabbing.

In *A Christmas Story*, the competitive spirit clutches the Old Man when he decides it's time to buy a Christmas tree. He wants to get to the lot early to purchase a superior one. He says to the rest of the Parker clan, "Get in the car. Get in the car. If we don't hurry, we're gonna miss all the good trees."

There is no major ethical issue with that; the most attractive trees do tend to sell first. Who wants a tree in their home that looks like a leftover? That's embarrassing when people visit for the holidays, no matter how well we try to hide holes and scraggly branches with ornaments—although, I've done it quite successfully. When I had little money during college, I was an expert at using fake icicles to hide my trees' flaws. Sometimes I could even acquire a leftover tree for free by waiting until late Christmas Eve, when the lots were abandoned.

The Old Man shops at the "Christmas-tree emporium of the entire Midwest," according to the proprietor. Quite a boast. We know right away that the seller is a cagey player in the Olympic sport of tree bargaining. The tree lot is this guy's own playing field; he knows the turf. But he might not play fair. Beware, Old Man! Watch the trees and your cash.

## Why Did Shepherd Want to Include the Tree-Shopping Scene?

According to Shepherd, competition is part of life, especially among men. The Old Man even feels that shopping for a tree is a competitive sport. He aims to outfox the Christmas-tree peddler, not just to purchase a decent tree. For him, it was like negotiating for a car; he was going to win the absolutely best deal he could by matching wits successfully with his opponent. His ego was at stake. So was his image with his family, who was witnessing his bargaining. He wasn't going to be improperly dishonest, but he was going to triumph with at least a win-win outcome.

Right away, the game is on, man to man, word to word, bluff to bluff. Seeing that he's got a serious buyer with his family in tow, the peddler shoots for a quick win: "Now, you ain't gonna find no better tree than this here tree. This here tree is built to last. Ain't no needles coming off this here tree." I love the phrase "built to last." Sounds like the tag line for the power drill I just received for Christmas. I wonder how long a tree would actually last in a Hammond-area house in 1940, with little humidity, and the tree wrapped in large, hot incandescent lights.

Then, of course, the seller pounds the tree on the ground and oodles of needles fall off, creating a green ring on the snow. The Old Man realizes that the seller is a second-rate pitchman, with whom he can definitely compete. The guy is bush league, compared to the Old Man's finely tuned rhetorical abilities and arboreal expertise.

In order to impress both his wife and the seller, the Old Man ramps up his demands: "Haven't you got a *big* tree?" In other words, the Old Man is serious. He's going to make a significant purchase, but the proprietor has to go along with the Old Man's self-boasting in order to make the deal in front of his family. We're not talking about an automobile or a boat—mere kid's stuff in the trading world. We're talking about haggling for a tree that will turn yellow in about three weeks.

The pitchman must offer something that will suggest the Old Man has got him cornered. The scruffy salesman says, "I'll knock off $2 because you're a man who knows his trees." That's it—some wonderful flattery to make the Old Man look respected in front of Mom and the kids. Maybe the seller is not quite as amateurish at bargaining as the Old Man initially assumed.

Not to let the tree impresario win back any turf on the playing field, however, the Old Man brilliantly whispers to Mom, in earshot of the peddler, that his pal just purchased "one of those brand-new, green plastic trees." It's a very savvy move, a bluff that the peddler has probably heard repeatedly but still has to take seriously. The peddler feels like he could lose the deal to a fake tree. Or is the Old Man bluffing? This is simply the way the tree-buying game is played—bluff to bluff. The tree might not be as fresh as the seller reports, and the Old Man might never buy a plastic tree. In fact, the Old Man winks at the seller.

The salesguy is still nervous. He needs to make the deal, fast, before the Old Man potentially sells his soul to an artificial tree store—maybe even Higbee's. The seller quickly ups his offer: "I'll throw in a rope and tie it to your car." The Old Man is pleased. He immediately exclaims, "You got a deal." What a great scene of fair play according to the rules of the game. Moreover, both sides are satisfied with the deal. Sure, there's a little puffery and deception along the way—but certainly within the rules of this kind of competition.

I once discovered on a Christmas-tree lot that the branches were extremely brittle and needles were falling off all of the trees. I asked the salesperson how long ago the trees had been cut down. "We just got them last week," he said, essentially avoiding my question. I looked more closely at one of the trees and discovered that it had been lightly spray-painted green. I figured that he was not bargaining fairly, so I went to a competing lot. I was delighted to have outfoxed a guy trying to con me; it made my day. "I won. I won. I won," as the Old Man says when he learns that he snagged the "major award."

Another situation involving potentially unfair play in *A Christmas Story* is the boy-to-boy competition on the school playground, leading up to Flick's unfortunate flagpole incident.

While walking to school, Schwartz reports to Ralphie and Flick, "I asked my old man about sticking your tongue to metal light poles in winter. And he says it will freeze right to the pole."

## Why Does Schwartz Say That Flick Is "Full of Beans"?

During the verbal sparring by the flagpole on the school playground, Schwartz says to Flick, "You're full of beans and so is your old man." Then there is the perfunctory who-says-so sparring. Shepherd loved etymology, and that phrase about beans is what Shepherd called a "doozy." Many scholars think the beans term came from the fourteenth-century phrase "full of prunes." And we know what prunes do to us—as do some beans.

Flick responds by playfully insulting Schwartz's father: "Ah, baloney. What would your old man know about anything?" Schwartz claims his father "saw a guy stick his tongue to a railroad track on a bet. And the fire department had to come to get the guy's tongue off the track." Okay, let's take that as an honest report from Schwartz, assuming his father was not spoofing him. Schwartz has some relatively solid but secondhand information to bargain with.

Schwartz quickly double dares Flick to put his tongue on the pole. Shep says, "The exact exchange and nuance of phrase in this ritual was very important." In other words, playing fair on the playground involves particular rules of etiquette.

Before long, Schwartz hits Flick with the expected "double-dog dare." Shep says the situation is now serious: "What else was left but a triple dare you?" At this point, Schwartz—impatiently and improperly—jumps right to what Shep calls the "coup de grâce—the sinister triple-dog dare."

Now, Schwartz is no longer playing fair. Shep tells us that Schwartz "created a slight breach of etiquette by skipping the triple dare and going right for the throat." The breach might indeed be "slight," but the consequences will be significant. There is no going back now; Cleveland Street history will have to take its course through the fate of irreversible childhood negotiation. A done dare is a done dare.

Maybe the two competitors would have ended up with the same result even if Schwartz had not violated custom. But perhaps even a slight delay in the dialogue, to cover the complete verbal protocol, would have resulted in the school bell ringing, aborting the entire fiasco. This is suggested in the movie because the bell goes off almost immediately after Flick gets his tongue stuck. There is no time to reconsider the deal or Flick's lingual difficulty. Life moves on at Warren G. Harding School.

In any case, Schwartz seemed determined from the beginning not to let Flick off the hook in their daring spars. Schwartz pressed swiftly, forcing Flick to try to offer any evidence that would disprove the claim by Schwartz *and* his father that tongues do stick to frozen metal. Family honor seems to be at stake, with the young Schwartz having to duel for himself and his dad. Flick seems to have no choice but to stick his warm, moist tongue on the frigid flagpole.

Also worthy of note is Shepherd's view of boys putting down their friends' fathers. Shepherd believed that this is fair game in friendly verbal jesting among boys. But as I indicate elsewhere, Shepherd also felt that it was unfair play for boys to criticize one another's mothers. So, he avoided it in his stories. In this case, the fact that Flick questioned the veracity of Schwartz's father is not really an issue of fair play.

Here's a tough one: Was it fair for Mom to push Ralphie to reveal where he learned the F-bomb, which he blurted out while helping the Old Man change the Oldsmobile's tire? Mom surely knew that the Old Man used the word regularly in front of Ralphie—even if not fully ten times daily, as Shep states hyperbolically. What are the fair rules for such engagement between mother and child—or, at least, between mother and son?

The Old Man swears—a lot. Yet Mom doesn't want Ralphie to swear. So, she's going to try to keep Ralphie from picking up her husband's bad verbal habits. Is that even possible? Shepherd felt that such tough parent-child sparring over proper language is simply what happens, regardless of whether or not it's fair or successful. Family relationships and parental discipline are messy. Parents have to do the best they can, given the circumstances. And children have to live with the results. There is little room for negotiation. But it's worth noting that the Old Man doesn't really discipline Ralphie for swearing. Is he a hypocrite?

What about the sparring between Mom and the Old Man over displaying the leg lamp in the front window? When the Parker clan leaves the house to go Christmas-tree shopping, a serious competition ensues. We know that Mom tried to talk to her husband about the issue during the grand unboxing, but he was too pridefully obsessed with his victory to listen. Therefore, Mom attempts a different tack, simply turning off the lamp when they leave the house. Her excuse? "Don't wanna waste electricity." She's a leg up on the Old Man as well as the green economy.

Shep describes what was going on when she turned off the lamp for that first time: "My mother was about to make another brilliant maneuver in the legendary battle of the lamp. The epic struggle which follows lives in the folklore of Cleveland Street to this very day." Again, in Shepherd's humor, small things offer big life lessons.

In other words, Mom was beginning a competition with the Old Man over who had the will, if not the power, to control how the family projected its morals as well as its aesthetics to the neighborhood. The lamp was at least implicitly sensual, not just ugly. These husband-wife skirmishes were about the family image as much as the Old Man's pride. Mom was trying to avoid family embarrassment, while the Old Man was aiming to proclaim to the world that he was a real winner in life, the recipient of a major award.

Would the Old Man be allowed to "turn on" the neighborhood, as Shep describes it? Or would Mom get to "turn off" the lamp and thereby save the family ethos? Mom is going to have to win if she wants to protect the Parker image. The Old Man, of course, is not interested in a compromise. He's playing self-righteously and pigheadedly, as if he didn't have any real competition. Mom is playing fair; the Old Man doesn't even want Mom on the playing field.

Shepherd told me that when he was growing up the father ruled the roost in nearly all neighborhood homes. By social protocol, the husband would have final say in such a leg-lamp battle. Mom would have to be subversive, undermining the standards of fair play in the context of those normally rigid family dynamics.

Today, marriages tend to be more egalitarian. Displaying a potentially offensive piece of "art" in a front window probably couldn't be mandated by either spouse.

The crisis in the battle comes when Mom reports, "I was watering my plant and broke your lamp." She sure did—and quite successfully! The Old Man loses his cool. It was not an accident. They both know it, according to my conversations with Shepherd. Once the Old Man refused to negotiate on placing the lamp in the front window, the result was inevitable. Only the kids don't know any better; they assume it was an accident. In their view, Mom would never intentionally destroy anything that meant a lot to someone else. She is a sweetie.

## Is the Leg Lamp a "Weed" in Mom's Garden?

This is so interesting! Mom breaks the lamp when she is watering her plant. Back in the day, house plants were not nearly so popular. And she needed to place the plant (which looks like a fern, one of the earth's oldest plant groups) where it would get light, by the same window where the lamp was carefully positioned by the Old Man. But once again, there are biblical echoes in this story. Mom is like Eve, tending to the garden that the Old Man has desecrated with his tawdry leg lamp. To her, the leg lamp is not "natural" and must be pulled out, like a weed.

The Old Man fumes, claiming that she was always jealous of the lamp, which apparently is his only major award (yet she was the one who knew the "Victor-the-horse" answer in order for him to win the contest). There's some crazy competitiveness! She's trying to defend the family image—or what's left of it, given the Old Man's ongoing battles with the Bumpus hounds and his unreliable Olds, which probably rumbles down the street like the clunker it is. He's actually set on protecting the always-fading image of his intelligence, or perhaps his entire manhood, by displaying a leg lamp.

It seems to me that Mom competed fairly in the face of the Old Man's unwillingness to work toward a win-win compromise. As soon as he placed the lamp in the front window for everyone else to observe and gossip about, without spousal discussion, he was taking his stand for once and all times. If the sexy lamp suddenly disappeared, neighbors might ask him what happened to it. By having to say that the lamp was moved elsewhere in the house, he would be admitting his lack of authority to dictate family life. Ironically—as irony emerges in nearly every scene of this movie—the Old Man will have to explain his loss, anyway. He becomes a real loser even though he's the "real" winner of the award.

What about fair play between the school kids and the bullies? We dislike Scut Farkus because he's a bully. By definition, bullies don't play fair. They intimidate people, threaten them, and find pleasure in making others' lives miserable. There is nothing virtuous about anything a bully does, except to cease being one. A redeemed bully is quite a wonderful outcome.

The apparent competition between Scut and Ralphie comes to a head because of Ralphie's emotional condition after receiving the poor grade on his theme, compounded by Miss Shields' warning about not shooting his eye out. Ralphie was not really looking to compete with Scut or his toady, Grover Dill. Avoidance was Ralphie's approach, and rightly so. There's no sense in trying to spar with nasty people who don't play fair.

Mom and the Old Man do find a compromise over Ralphie's special, handmade gift from Aunt Clara—the outlandish bunny pajamas. The Old Man empathizes with Ralphie's embarrassment. After all, the bunny getup is a real affront to Ralphie's emerging manhood. Ralphie doesn't want to put it on. He even fears that if Flick witnesses him in the garish garb, it will make his life in the neighborhood and at school a "veritable hell." Shep tells us, capturing young Ralphie's perspective as he models the outfit on the stairs' landing, "My feet began to sweat as those two fluffy little bunnies with the blue button eyes stared sappily up at me." The Old Man doesn't want Ralphie to have to wear the humiliating costume, ever. The Old Man isn't the most empathetic guy in the world, but he can imagine himself as Ralphie, putting on the most unmanly pajamas.

The Old Man eventually asserts his authority in tune with Ralphie's manly feelings. But he has to do so carefully, knowing that Mom is protecting her sister's honor. Mom realizes that loving Ralphie means considering her son's feelings, but she still wants to honor Clara. She says that Ralphie will only have to wear the outfit when Aunt Clara visits. Done deal! A win-win outcome.

Shepherd believed that there is something basic in human nature that inclines us to favor fairness over unfairness. Moreover, we can easily develop resentments toward people who don't treat us fairly. We want to be treated fairly, according to the Golden Rule of treating others the way we would want to be treated.

Some of our everyday competition is just playful—like determining who knows more about cars or sports. And there are established rules of the game for things like "daring" competitions. When the Old Man battles the tree salesman, the two of them wonderfully play by the rules of such competition, expecting and accepting a bit of bluffing. That could be a model for life. We accept a bit of "normal" bluffing toward the goal of everyone leaving the deal a "winner."

Maybe there should be rules about fair play for interspousal competitions as well. Mom and the Old Man needed such rules to guide their battle over displaying the lamp. But the underlying problem in that case is disquieting: The Old Man—the great Arab tree bargainer—would not really listen to Mom's concern and give her an equal role on the playing field. Playing fair requires all of us to respect our everyday competitors—as we expect of all good sports in the game of life.

## CHAPTER 12

# Hold Your Tongue

**W**hen actor Peter Billingsley uttered the famous F-bomb in *A Christmas Story* while helping the Old Man change the Oldsmobile's tire, he didn't say "fudge." Really. For that important scene, with the crew listening, he verbalized *the* "F" word, repeatedly. Of course, to avoid offending the movie audience, Ralphie's audio is changed to a drawn-out "fuuuuudge." We all know what he purportedly said.

One of the recurring topics in *A Christmas Story* is "swearing"—such as obscenity, profanity, and other potentially offensive language. Swearing is sprinkled throughout the film, creating a sense of emerging middle-class culture (one generation removed, but still shaped by the ways of a working-class family). The "F" word, however, is off-limits in the PG-rated movie (and there was no PG-13 rating in 1983, when the movie was released).

*A Christmas Story* raises issues about when swearing is appropriate. No one in the movie seems to think that Ralphie's use of the real F-bomb during the tire-changing scene is proper—even the Old Man, who apparently used the word regularly in front of the family yet whispers it in Mom's ear to inform her what Ralphie said as Randy tries to listen in.

As I mentioned earlier, swearing in the movie is portrayed as an art form of sorts. Shep says, "My father worked in profanity the way other artists might work in oils or clay. It was his true medium. A master."

This is not just a joke about the Old Man's language. Jean Shepherd is depicting a culture that includes various habits, rituals, and male sparring. To swear well—creatively and impressively—was part of the way men earned their rank in the masculine pecking order when they were alone together. Their wives or girlfriends might not even know how crude their language could be in such situations.

In *A Christmas Story*, Shepherd is not trying to be crudely funny like a foulmouthed club comic. He told me that many comics rely on obscene language because their stories and other material are not really funny; they try to shock audiences by employing language that most people don't hear regularly in public. I watched one of the comedy channels on TV and discovered exactly what Shepherd meant—a lot of rough language with weak attempts at humor.

I had a similar conversation with Jerry Seinfeld, who said that Shepherd was the greatest influence on his own comic sensibilities. Authentic, situational humor doesn't require coarse language to be funny. Coarse language would not have added any comedic value to the *Seinfeld* TV show if it had been on cable TV rather than on broadcast TV, where the standards are stricter. Situational humor based on everyday life requires a lot more creative effort.

In fact, the F-bomb scene in *A Christmas Story* is funnier because we *don't* hear Ralphie speak the word. The use of the drawn-out "fuuuuudge" is far wittier—not just less offensive for parents who might be watching the movie with younger children.

Shepherd uses swearing in the movie partly to get at the moral tension between appropriate and inappropriate language in everyday life. The fact that Shepherd and director Bob Clark were able to do this in an otherwise family-oriented film that appeals to a broad range of viewers is a mark of their sensitivity to the issues involved.

Like Shepherd, I grew up in a Chicago-area, lower-middle-class family and heard swearing from the time I could crawl. During high school, I got a job in a printing plant that really exposed me to the kind of tapestries of obscenity and profanity woven by the Old Man. I was a bit shocked, even though I knew the language. The guys working there really did spar over who could outswear the others. One of them joked in front of the group that I was so skinny I was going to fall through my a--hole and hang myself. Everyone howled with delight. I have to admit, it was a wildly comical image.

In the film, Shepherd's life lesson is that although swearing can be a kind of art form in some social circles, we all need to learn how to hold our tongues. Not all language fits every situation, even if the language is clever or impresses some listeners. Moreover, he shows that crude language isn't always funny. Shepherd also suggests that we need women, most of all, to help men learn this life lesson about holding our tongues. Even in this book, I wanted to "censor" swearing to avoid offending young readers.

As Shepherd told me, some men try to prove their manhood by spewing nasty language whenever they feel that a person, an organization (like the government or a business), or thing is challenging them. In the movie, we are introduced to the Old Man's verbal artistry when he admits that his beloved Olds is really a "[g-d-d---ed] pile of junk." Shepherd's use of the "GD" term here is not merely for authenticity; the Old Man's car is truly "da--able," unredeemable. He's tired of dealing with a "son of a b----" that would "freeze up in the middle of the summer in the equator." The language fits both the Old Man's anger toward the vehicle and Shepherd's use of hyperbole to make a point. Mom would never use such vulgarity, and she doesn't want her sons to hear it let alone employ it.

## Why Do Moms Care More Than Dads about Nasty Language?

In the movie, Mom warns the Old Man to watch his swearing in front of Ralphie and Randy. She offers the "little pitchers [have big ears]" line—a classic reminder in many homes, used almost exclusively by women to curtail male verbal excess. It's like saying to the Old Man, "Hey, watch it, potty mouth! Do you really want our kids to learn that?" But why do moms care more about this issue than dads? According to Shepherd, swearing is part of the male nature, one form of bravado as well as artistry.

In my experience growing up in Chicago, it was more common to hear both the swearing and the subsequent warnings in homes with only sons. Having even one daughter in the house created a different sense of domestic propriety.

Immediately following the auto-related swearing, the furnace goes into "clinker" mode, capturing the Old Man's entire attention as well as his linguistic imagination. He must enter the battle, with suitable language to express both his frustration and his machismo against the forces of darkness in the cellar. For a few moments, he heeds Mom's advice: "That blasted stupid furnace. Dadgummit." When he's out of sight, on the way down the stairs to enter battle, however, he encounters the "d--- skates." He's off to the verbal races, swearing up a firestorm that drifts upstairs with the smoke.

All heck is about to break loose verbally—to put it mildly. There is no cap on the Old Man's mouth when he engages the dark enemy below. But first he has to communicate directly with Mom, within earshot of Ralphie and Randy. So, he yells upstairs, "Oh, for 'cripes sake' [he might say something more offensive, although it's hard to tell in the audio], open up the damper, will you? Who the h--- turned it all the way down again?"

Director Clark and actor Darren McGavin transform the Old Man's unbridled, furnace-fighting swearing into laughable gibberish. It sounds something like, "blurred, rattle, crash, camel flirt." He continues with fuming poetry that resembles, "Gollywop-dopter-crop-dop-fratenhouse-stickelfeiffer." We all can imagine swearing along the lines of what he's saying, but the director avoids using language that would offend viewers as well as be too specific to be humorous. This makes the Old Man's alleged poetic exclamations even funnier as well as fitting for a family audience.

## What Do Ralphie and the Old Man Really Say When Swearing?

In tune with the movie's PG rating, Shepherd and director Bob Clark used gibberish to capture the more extravagant episodes of swearing. Actor Darren McGavin (the Old Man) invented his own strings of gibberish when battling the furnace. Actor Peter Billingsley (Ralphie) used scripted gibberish when fighting bully Scut Farkus.

Shep tells us more about the Old Man's amazing, macho linguistic feats: "In the heat of the battle, my father wove a tapestry of obscenity that, as far as we know, is still hanging in space over Lake Michigan." Brilliant! Here's the legendary Parker artiste weaving strings of foul verses. His tapestries were so amazingly innovative that they made lasting contributions to the art of cursing in the Midwest. Some classical art will hang on display for centuries in the Art Institute of Chicago, across the lake. Other art will hover forever like eternal drones over the big lake, heard by boaters as eerie echoes of ancient civilizations' male bravado.

Meanwhile, linguistic neophyte Ralphie and his pals are learning how to practice the art of swearing as a means of impressing one another with their emerging manhood. Swearing comes with the relevant male hormones, a kind of budding machismo. Nothing they are able to say so far in their lives will reach the pantheon of poetry to compete with the Old Man's linguistic tapestries. The boys are mere novices.

The bathroom scene, where Ralphie is embarrassed as well as disappointed by the "crummy" Ovaltine commercial, is a case in point. Little Orphan Annie and her coconspirators have pulled the wool over Ralphie's eyes. Ralphie believed that he was being inducted into a special group of secret decoders. After all, he had spent "weeks . . . drinking gallons of Ovaltine in order to get the Ovaltine inner seal" to send off for his decoder ring.

But as it turns out, marketing masterminds were just fooling him. He has been had. Understandably, he borrows from the less-developed section of his Old Man's rich vocabulary of responses to life's irritations, whispering the SOB term so Mom can't hear it outside the closed bathroom door, where Randy is waiting desperately to relieve himself.

Ralphie and his pals face a real dilemma while ramping up their mannish lingo. They want to act like men, especially to impress each other. They are learning the craft primarily by listening to their fathers. At the same time, they don't want to risk punishment by offending their mothers and other females. Neither do they want to snitch on each another for using foul language. So, they have to practice swearing confidentially among one another, being mindful of anyone in earshot, and not uttering such words impulsively when they get heated.

Shepherd paints a picture of men protecting men in their use of swearwords. Ralphie "chickened out," says Shep, when he could have reported to Mom that he actually learned the F-bomb primarily from the Old Man.

Still, the manly swearing club always has its internal tensions. It's tough to impress one another and yet hold back as necessary, when those outside the club are within earshot. In times of battle with cars, furnaces, and people, men easily disregard social proprieties. They just seem unable to help it, particularly when their flared tempers automatically emit raw language.

This happens when Ralphie engages bully Scut Farkus in hand-to-hand combat. Again, we viewers are not privy to the specific language. We do know from Shep, however, that something switched in the "recesses" of Ralphie's brain. A "tiny, red-hot little flame began to grow." Finally, as Shep tells us, "Something had happened. A fuse blew and I had gone out of my skull."

The result was not just Ralphie's physical attack on bully Scut. Ralphie digs deep into his growing lexicon of swearwords to come up with doozies that shock the developing crowd of wide-eyed, open-eared observers around the makeshift boxing ring—including Randy. "Did you hear what he said?" says one kid at the scene. Schwartz adds, "Holy smokes." Shep says that a "torrent of obscenities and swearing of all kinds was pouring out" of Ralphie as he "screamed." Some of those tapestries might still be floating over Lake Michigan, underneath the Old Man's elevated weavings.

## Are Men Quick to Speak— before Thinking?

Shepherd's view of men was fairly bleak. Among other problems, males are supposedly more inclined to quickly say things that they will regret. In the process of impressing one another, men also violate the norms of generally appropriate language. According to Shepherd, this seems to be a primordial issue, not just a matter of culture. Men tend to be nasty yellers. Crude put-down artists. Fabricators of outrageous language, even if it's somewhat poetic. Men habitually insert their feet in their mouths.

Is there hope for men in their struggle to hold their tongues? Should they even try?

Perhaps, with the moderating effect of women on them, men can temperately self-regulate their crude vocabularies as appropriate. After Mom breaks the leg lamp, says Shep, the furious Old Man "stood quivering with fury, stammering, as he tried to come up with a real crusher." But all he was willing to say was, "Not a finga!" Such amazing linguistic control! He could let loose on the furnace and the car, but he knew better than to use his offensive vocal tapestries to crush his wife. That was off-limits—even though Mom had "crushed" his lamp.

As the movie moves toward its magical Christmas Day scenes, the males do hold their tongues better than in earlier sections of the film. The most the Old Man can muster, even when he loses his precious turkey to the Bumpus bloodhounds, is, "Sons of bi-----! Bumpuses!" He chokes on the insult at the back door, not even loud enough for the Bumpuses or other neighbors to hear. It was a rather mild put-down, given the Old Man's ravenous desire to eat the freshly basted, golden-brown turkey slathered with gravy. He had been salivating like one of Pavlov's dogs all morning. When it came to swearing where his entire family could hear it on Christmas morning, however, even his Pavlovian response was considerably attenuated.

Even in the emerging middle-class neighborhoods where I was raised, swearing was reserved largely for males to vent and to compete in their own macho world. In Shepherd's view, human beings are blessed with one sex (women) who are called to keep the other sex (men) from spinning out of linguistic control. We all have to hold our tongues, using fitting language in order to  avoid offending others and escalating potential conflicts. But without women, men seem to be in deeper verbal doodoo. Oh, Fudgsicles®!

## CHAPTER 13

# Be Playful

In a scene from *A Christmas Story* that is seemingly disconnected from the main plotlines of the film, Ralphie's entire class puts wax fangs in their mouths at the beginning of class. What a wonderful prank! Of course, Miss Shields has to act like she's displeased, but is probably chuckling to herself. She holds out her hand for the class to file by and relinquish their fake teeth.

The camera shows us her dedicated desk drawer, filled with kids' sundry, amusing items that probably helped classmates and Miss Shields giggle through the daily grind of teaching and learning. One set of windup teeth that's already in the drawer still clacks when jostled.

Not to be outdone by Miss Shields' students, I bought and distributed wax fang teeth to my university students just before Jean Shepherd arrived to give a lecture one day. When Shepherd looked up from the desk, where he sat to dispense his wisdom, he saw what Miss Shields witnessed—a knockoff scene from his own film!

Shepherd cracked up. As we all did. It was a great class session. No, Shepherd didn't ask the students to come forward to hand over their fangs. The students could take them home as a memento of the time they pranked a mischief-maker with his own scheme.

## Is Humor Fun—and Fun Humorous?

Shepherd considered himself a storytelling humorist, not just a one-line comedian. He aimed to make *A Christmas Story* a funny set of stories from beginning to end. In his worldview, humor is natural fun, even when it involves "serious" matters. He believed that without a sense of humor, we can't really enjoy life. So, even when he tells scary or distressing tales, he wants to capture the underlying humor. For instance, we might laugh even when we hear Schwartz's mother on the phone punishing him (mistakenly) for passing along the "F" word to Ralphie. Such irony is a difficult way to convey the "humor" in a serious situation. What about the fight scene? What is "humorous" about it? Is it more than kids' play? Certainly it's not just funny.

In the movie, Mom and the Old Man are dealing with young Randy's reluctance to eat dinner. It was an enduring issue in the Parker household. As Shep puts it, "My kid brother had not eaten voluntarily in over three years." Quite a record; about half his life. Nearly as noteworthy as the losing streaks of the Chicago White Sox and Bears during the same period. It's also surprising that the Old Man even noticed what was happening with Randy at the table; his nose was perennially stuck in a newspaper while he was masticating his meat loaf.

But what can we do as parents when even catsup or another sweet or salty product is an insufficient additive to the grub that kids refuse to consume? Should we force them to sit at the table until they give in? Imagine eating cold tongue two hours later! I did it, one tiny, squishy bite at a time, washed down my gullet with room-temperature milk. I couldn't leave the table until I had finished. That was an inescapable rule.

The battle between parents and children over the domestic menu calls for creativity on both sides. My sister-in-law admits that she hated overcooked peas so much that she would clandestinely squish them into the cracks between the main table and the hanging table leaves in order to pretend that she had consumed them. Sometimes the dog would lick them out from underneath. Dogs are our best friends for numerous reasons.

Probably all parents have tried this kind of gut-wrenching, world-class appeal to a headstrong kid: "Starving people would be happy to have that," Mom says to Randy while he plays with his meat loaf, mashed potatoes, and red cabbage—whimpering along the way as a musical accompaniment to his dramatic displeasure.

Expressing disapproval about dinner cuisines has probably created more tuneful versions of kid whimpering than all other stimulants combined. It's an art form in itself. If we add the facial expressions to the whimpers, we have a full-bodied theatrical genre. I bet some communication professor has authored a doctoral dissertation, "Varieties of Nonverbal and Verbal Expression among Food-Averse Children as a Mealtime Ritual in Modern America."

The Old Man chimes in, "Can I have some more red cabbage." He's unappreciatively just shoveling his chow down his throat while Randy is pushing it around his plate, building a meat-and-potatoes tower on a vertically planted fork, with an impressive parapet placed elegantly at the peak. It was Randy's own Tower of Babel, a way to make a name for himself as a connoisseur of gastronomic art. And just as the Babylonians ignored God, Randy doesn't listen to the Old Man's warnings.

Perhaps no normal father can handle a reluctant eater for too long, assuming he occasionally peeks around his newspaper to catch up on the latest table antics. Paternal impatience eventually sets in, fueled by simmering annoyance. The Old Man tells Randy, "You stop playing with your food, or I'll give you something to cry about. You better stop fooling around with that and eat it, or you'll be sorry."

What kind of impact do such dire threats actually have when they are delivered nightly with few consequences? Randy is just Randy, a budding monk who can survive on milk and honey (or sugar cookies). The Old Man is the Old Man—a big talker who thinks he's in control of mealtime while he reads the dismal Chicago sports-team rankings at the table. He seems to have lost his sense of humor on both counts.

People commonly say we shouldn't play with our food. Okay, there are times and places when doing so would be inappropriate—such as going out to a restaurant or to a stuffy relative's house for dinner. The playful sister-in-law I mentioned earlier likes to recount how she flipped an olive from her French sauce spoon into her uppity aunt's wine glass at their linen-clothed dining table. It was quite a shot—a three-pointer. It also led to a new tiki bar drink—a one-balled chardonnay.

Shepherd's life lesson challenges the don't-play-with-your-food adage, literally and figuratively. There is something much more going on at the Parker dinner table than Randy's reluctance to eat. There is no fun. No joy. Not even conversation. The mealtime is simply too functionally mundane.

Shepherd captures an interesting and perhaps controversial life lesson: We should be playful in life—even if means lightheartedly challenging social etiquette sometimes. His point is that we can take social rules too far. We can become legalistic, as if rigid social norms are a basis for enjoying life. We create unhealthy social environments that rob us of the joy of play, including lightheartedly breaking the rules.

## Should Fashion Be Fun?

I recall talking about social etiquette with Shepherd, who liked to dress a bit too modish, in my opinion. When leisure suits were popular, he would wear a semigarish one with broader and longer collars than normal. He said, "Look, Quin, when you're playing college football, you have to follow the rules. The same for doing business deals. But too many people don't enjoy life because they're constantly worried about doing something wrong. They act like they're unhappy about everything. About life itself." Shepherd was addressing our tendency to be so straitlaced that we rob our lives of fun. We forget how to play—even with fashion. We become boring people living tedious lives where everyone is uptight about not offending others.

Randy, the dinnertime poet of whining, actually elevates the playful table discourse: "Meat loaf, smeet loaf, double beetloaf." It's a funny rhyme, artsy in its own right. Why get irritated at him for such creative juices? Keep going, Randy! How about adding "creep loaf" or "feet loaf"? The Old Man might teasingly say, "Stop your weep loaf and eat your doggone meat loaf. I'll toss you to the Bumpus hounds if you don't start shoveling it down. They'll lick you silly."

Still, no one at the table is smiling. Tension grows among the Parker clan as Randy digs in to his antifood stance in the nondebate. It's a standoff. The rules of the table game have run their course.

Finally, Randy reveals the heart of the matter for him: "I hate meat loaf." Why would that be, other than the fact that the Parkers consumed it nightly throughout his life—with cold leftover slabs plastered on lunchtime sandwiches made with spongy white bread devoid of whole-grain crunchiness? Also, kids tend to get bored with nearly any routine. Where's the fun in one more, predictable meat loaf serving? How about some "sweetloaf"—whatever that would be? Maybe meat loaf fried like French toast, smothered with butter, and sprinkled with powdered sugar? Makes me salivate, just thinking about it.

Randy pushes the Old Man to the breaking point: "All right, I'll get that kid to eat [note: not "my son," but "that kid"]. Where's my screwdriver and my plumber's helper? I'll open up his mouth and shove it in." Every father has thought about doing something like this, naturally with tools, to force-feed a stubborn kiddo. This is bravado talk. It makes the Old Man feel good, like he's actually in charge. But, of course, he's totally unpersuasive as well as comical.

Mom steps up to the plate as only mothers typically can. They don't see the situation as a war between kid and parents as much as a muffled love affair with a temporarily fussy child. Time for charm. For humor. For a little play. For female coaxing. After all, Randy is a kid; threats and logic are not likely to convince him of anything when just food is at stake. He knows he won't be starved! And he could continue playing with his food all evening, creating a plate full of new highways and byways as well as impressive edifices. The Tower of Babel is just the beginning. Next up is the entire Methodist church complex down the street, with a Randy-designed, forked steeple that looks like a devil's pitchfork.

"How do the little piggies go?" Mom asks Randy, lightheartedly. He knows the answer from all of the Golden Books, nursery rhymes, and petting-farm visits: "Oink, oink." Brilliant, Randy!

"Now," challenges eloquent Mom, "show me how the piggies eat." She points to Randy's plate: "This is your trough. Show me how the piggies eat. Be a good boy. Show Mommy how the piggies eat." Dazzlingly persuasive rhetoric! Randy gets to play rather than simply force the fare down his throat. He gets to fool around with his food! This is truly the life for a young kid who is bored out of his mind with beetloaf.

## Why Is *A Christmas Story* Trivia So Much Fun?

Shepherd loved using trivia in his stories, partly because he was a trivia buff. He said that interesting trivia engages audiences and keeps them rewatching the same movie—and encourages family members to compete over trivia knowledge. The best movie trivia, he said, was real-life references from the past that still resonate today. For instance, suppose the Old Man's newspaper contest asks the following question: "Who's the most famous pig in the world?" This question is part of the annual "Greatest Film Stars in American History" series, guaranteed to give away at least one "major award." The answer: Porky. Really. Porky Pig first appeared on the big screen in 1935 and became the longest-running Looney Tunes figure of all time. As the Old Man ponders the question, Randy says, "Dat's all folks!" Mom then gets the answer, but the Old Man misses it. Great fun!

The Parkers' situation reminds me of trying to get my toddler grandson to eat plain, sugar-free, colorless yogurt—the healthful but tasteless kind. He didn't even want to try the sample that I scooped into a bowl colored with cartoon characters. He clamped down his teeth when I offered a pink spoonful. We were immediately at a stalemate. The last thing I wanted to do was get angry with him. Besides, I doubted I would have eaten the same stuff when I was his age, although we never ate anything fancy like yogurt back then.

The plastic yogurt container was still on the dining table, near his high-chair tray. I dipped my pinky into the container and licked some of the creamy stuff off my finger. He giggled as he watched me, like I was being silly. I did it again. He laughed louder. I dipped my pinky into the yogurt container a third time and offered my pinky to him, right in front of his mouth. He looked at it, looked at me, giggled, and then licked the bland yogurt off my finger. Then he giggled yet again. Done deal. For months, he loved eating yogurt right out of the carton, with his own fingers. He would giggle even when he saw me taking the yogurt container out of the refrigerator.

In *A Christmas Story*, however, the Old Man is not interested in any culinary fun. He's a no-nonsense guy, bent on forcing submission to proper etiquette (even though he breaks other etiquette, such as swearing around the house in front of the kids). While Randy begins eating like a piggy, the Old Man offers an "O, my G-d" under his breath. Then he refocuses on the newspaper, but if he's reading actual news, those reports deserve his lord-help-us remark more than do Randy's plate antics. The Old Man can't figure out why his manly dictates and direct threats aren't effective. He seems clueless about play. He's a tool guy—no matter what the problem. He thinks crowbars, not laughter.

Randy sticks his face into the culinary mishmash and starts gobbling up the swill in his trough. Randy and Mom are roaring with laughter. Ralphie is not so sure; he's not yet a man, but he's picking up manly skepticism about play from his father. Randy is giggling joyously, snorting like a pig, not just consuming meat loaf like one.

We increasingly tend to think of "family fun" as planned activities. Shepherd believed that fun often is spontaneous, like kids playing in the backyard, doing what comes naturally to them. Unplanned family play is a great gift. It can cut through the stresses of everyday domestic life. When we laughingly play together, we love together. We accept each other as we are, imperfect but cherished individuals brought together to enjoy one another's company and even to poke fun at social etiquette. Shepherd grew up without much of this kind of fun and used the writing of his stories vicariously as a way of breathing childlike fun into his own life.

Go for it, Randy! Make us all giddy with laughter about ourselves and the human condition. Oink about the Old Man's feigned manliness and Mom's dearest piggy coaxing. Help us to not take ourselves so seriously. We don't need a screwdriver and plumber's helper to transform a routine dinner into a taste of good-humored family life. We just require some fun, a new story we can tell each other from generation to generation: The day a ravenous piggy arrived at the Parker family trough and devoured Randy's plate-topping Tower of Babel.

Shepherd encourages us to be playful humorists rather than rigid killjoys. Humorous, etiquette-bending play can be a family affair—a tie that knits all of us into tapestries of cheer in a world of fear and anxiety.

Shepherd used to tell me that you can laugh or cry about everyday life, depending on how you look at it. But it's the humble humor in life, our down-to-earthness, our willingness to put our faces into the troughs together, that remind us how amazing everyday existence really is. We flourish when we

give up trying to force-feed life, including what the kids will eat, and instead playfully celebrate what lies right before us. That's life-affirming humor.

Even adults don't like or just get tired of particular foods—like Brussels sprouts. We are all at the same, human table. We need rules for living, but some social etiquette is best playfully challenged—at least when the rules are begging to be chewed up.

I doubt any amount of etiquette-breaking humor would have gotten me to enjoy eating tongue for dinner. There are limits. But I, for one, am going to continue eating yogurt with my finger, even when my grandson isn't around. And I might even do it while watching a Porky Pig cartoon. Oink, oink!

## CHAPTER 14

# Appreciate Your Daily Bread

I was out for coffee with Jean Shepherd on a cold winter morning in Michigan. It felt good just to get indoors at a warm diner. We stomped snow off of our shoes, took seats at a booth, and put in our orders: black coffee, straight up, for Jean; coffee with cream, for me.

The coffee arrived at our table, steaming hot, in white mugs. Shepherd looked down at his cup, smelled the aroma, took a quick sip, and said, "Quin, you know when you taste a good cup of coffee that there has to be a God." I responded, "Amen."

I said "Amen" as a reference to prayer—to the Lord's Prayer: "Give us this day our daily bread." Shepherd got it. That section of the Lord's Prayer is a declaration of dependence. We all depend on others to make our lives happen. I don't know who invented or first roasted coffee beans, but I'm grateful.

In the Bible lands of the Middle East, you had to have bread; it was a staple food, the nourishment for everyday life. On that day with Shepherd, our bread was a good cup of coffee.

One of the most intriguing life lessons in *A Christmas Story* is that we should appreciate our daily bread, however simple. Shepherd meant not just food—though that's the metaphor he uses—but all of the "stuff" of life that keeps us going and gives us physical, relational, and even spiritual sustenance.

In Shepherd's view, there was something sacramental about truly home-cooked foods such as meat loaf, pie, and grilled corn on the cob slobbered with butter. A grilled hamburger is fine. But baking meat loaf is more of a home-cooked art. Every family concocts it differently, sometimes with bread crumbs or raw eggs kneaded into it. I can imagine that the varieties of American meat loaf rival the various leavened and unleavened breads in the Middle East.

I've had meat loaf smothered with different catsups and BBQ sauces. I once had it topped with sliced tomatoes and basil pesto, but that was too "high church" for me personally—like serving a $180 bottle of cabernet at the Lord's Supper.

Sure, meat loaf is processed meat—not as "pure" as a steak. But as far as I know, meat loaf is made with beef. It's fairly simple to make and it smells great while baking in the oven. The Bumpus hounds would have gone after meat loaf on the Parker kitchen table. And I bet the Old Man salivates as he smells meat loaf cooking, day after day.

Probably like Mom in the movie, my mother made ground beef for meat loaf with an old hand grinder that bracketed on the side of our mustard-hued, linoleum kitchen table. I remember the crunching sound when she hit a piece of bone. I also recall how the grinder bracket would loosen up and the whole mechanism and its meaty contents would fall to the linoleum floor, where our dog, Spotty, was waiting, licking her chops. I never helped my mother grind the beef because I feared getting my fingers stuck in the gears.

The Parker family in *A Christmas Story* doesn't live high on the hog. They are common people in an emerging middle-class neighborhood pursuing a fairly simple way of life, with plenty of meat loaf. There are few knickknacks around the house. No impressive artwork on the walls.

## Are the Parkers' Colorful Dishes from the Era?

The Parker dishes are Fiestaware®, a colorful ceramic-glazed dishware that was popular during the movie's approximate time period. You can still find the originals at thrift shops today, or join the throngs of *A Christmas Story* fans who buy the updated styles from the revived company, which rightly calls the dishware "An American Icon." I bought a boxful of the original Fiestaware® when I was a college student setting up an apartment. I thought it was modernistically cool. Not expensive. Functional with great color. Back then, I thought—like Shepherd—that dishes should be enjoyable, not just functional. Why not set the everyday table with the same spirit we put into party planning?

The kitchen is bare bones, with checkered linoleum flooring, wood paneling halfway up the walls to the chair molding, the usual sugar and flour containers, straight-backed wooden chairs without cushions, a refrigerator, a breadbox, a stove, and an AM radio. Everyone in our neighborhood had such a radio; they all hummed irritatingly while playing Chicago's WGN—named after the humble 'tag line for the

*Chicago Tribune*, the "world's greatest newspaper." What the Parkers had in their kitchen was basic, "daily life" stuff—like the daily bread of meat loaf.

The only slightly more upscale item in the Parker home is the Maytag clothes wringer. It signified that Mom would be spending most of her time either cooking or doing laundry in the same room. That was fine, because the kitchen was the most important room in the house—long before the big, comfy kitchens of today. It was the spot for kibbitzing with family or neighbors.

Ralphie and his kin didn't have a family room, which was more of an upper-middle-class luxury. Their living room was so small that it could barely support the Christmas tree, the gifts, and the discarded wrapping paper tossed chaotically all over the floor on Christmas morning. "My G-d, would you look at that mess," says the Old Man after the end of that morning's gift-giving "bacchanalia" (a word used near the beginning of the film to capture all of the indulgent shopping and gift-giving). Still, Randy, his toy zeppelin in hand, had no trouble dozing off in the middle of the disarray, like a caged hamster using paper scraps for bedding.

In that tiny living-room space, the now-buried leg lamp was a monumental light—a real "statue," to quote the Old Man in his ecstatic unboxing. It's hard to imagine how Mom could have put up with the constant, room-dominating, sexy glow of the fish-net-clad leg in the Parker's cramped living room.

The movie captures an era when daily life was relatively uncomplicated, with one family car and no televisions or computers. Life revolved around the rituals of everyday activities, such as driving to and from work, running back and forth to school, listening to the radio, catching up on the news and sports with a daily, carrier-delivered newspaper, and gathering together for meals at a table rather than at a quick-come-and-go kitchen counter. School sports and other extracurricular activities were not yet beckoning so many children away from family dinners.

## Is *A Christmas Story* "Nostalgia"?

As I explained in the introduction, Shepherd never saw his screen-play or the resulting movie as mere nostalgia; he even called the movie "antinostalgic." Why? Because he knew that life was hard back in the 1940 era, just like it is today. As I argued with him, however, he agreed that the film does depict a simpler time, when most American homes were small and unadorned, and meat loaf was a domestic specialty, well appreciated. Fast-food restaurants were at best an entrepreneurial dream. In short, life was hard but probably less complicated than it is today. So, I enjoy the film for this sense of nostalgia.

For Shepherd, *A Christmas Story* is partly a tale about most Americans' "daily bread." It's not a film about social elites, the politically influential, or the people living in what he called "Westchester County" (a reference to the upper crust living north of New York City in spacious homes with family rooms, private wooded lots, and multicar garages). Shepherd didn't identify with such affluent people, including Hollywood celebrities. And he believed that such well-to-do people didn't appreciate his storytelling because they couldn't identify with common folks. (I tried to talk him out of that misconception.) He used to joke that naturally neurotic elites read John Updike rather than his novels.

In any case, meat loaf, for Shepherd, was not just a food. It was a symbol of a sufficient life. Of good, honest, working people. In Shepherd's mind, meat loaf was like the coffee he and I enjoyed together at the diner. It was a gift, worthy of enjoying without boasting about how much it cost or how it could be jazzed up with different flavors, like a mocha Frappuccino or a pumpkin spice latte. I think about this when I hear Jerry Seinfeld's bit about Pop-Tarts. They are not a fancy food, but they are simple and delicious—and at least as nutritious as the cardboard box in which they are packed, shipped, and stored. Manna? Not really. But a taste of it, maybe.

Meat loaf is meat loaf. It's one form of humankind's "daily bread," the good-but-not-fancy sustenance that we all require to live. In other words, we humans are called to spend time at home, office, school, or play, and then gather for our daily meat loaf. If such simple, meat loaf–loving people drink wine, it's, as the Old Man says on Christmas, probably "not bad" and "not good either."

My father had what he thought was a God-provided food too— Limburger cheese. We were poor, but he scrimped to be able to buy his blessed limburger. It came in a foil wrap that could never be tightly resealed once it was opened. The pungent smell of that heady stuff permeated the inside of our clanking refrigerator. You could not open the refrigerator door without getting a whiff of the noxious odor even in adjacent rooms. No one complained openly to him about the exotic bouquet, which to me seemed like the smell of gas after eating raw cauliflower. It was just a "dad thing." He loved it, almost like it had a holy significance for him—his nightly beer-and-limburger cheese "communion."

The Old Man in *A Christmas Story* likes his meat loaf. The Parker family eats pans of it. In fact, hearty meat loaf seems to be the only non-breakfast food they consume except for holidays (turkey on Christmas and perhaps ham on Easter), or when going out unexpectedly (duck at a Chinese restaurant). Add some mashed potatoes and red cabbage to the meat loaf, and the Parker clan had a sustaining meal of classic comfort food. It was like a domestic diner.

## Is Eating a Spiritual as Well as Physical Activity?

Shepherd, like an anthropologist, saw religious aspects of just about every human ritual. Eating meals is one of them. For him, our daily bread is physical and spiritual. While eating together, we are sustained by the love that can and sometimes does transcend our worries. We can taste a cup of coffee and give thanks for it—and really savor it, one sip at a time. The same is true for meat loaf. And when we are able to appreciate such signs of our daily bread with others, our joy in life is more complete. Even just having a family—which we might take for granted—is daily bread. Each in their own ways, the individual Parker family members help sustain the others, often at the table. They break bread together amid their fears and frustrations as well as their delights.

Here in West Michigan, part of my daily bread is sunshine. I never take it for granted. Winters can be brutal—weeks without bright sunlight. It wears me down emotionally. When the sun comes out, I beam. I feel rejuvenated, like the sense of delight while eating a great meal.

One January here in lake-effect snow country, Shepherd and I were teaching a course together. There was no sunlight, day after day, for three weeks. Only cloud cover and unrelenting lake-effect snow. It was also frigid, continually below freezing.

When I took Shepherd to the airport so he could fly home to Florida, he said something like, "Well, good luck, Quin. I don't know how the h--- you do it." I don't know, either. The drive home from the airport was a slip-and-slide adventure amid squalls delivering horizontal snowflakes the size of quarters. But we Michiganders do it, winter after winter. We play winter sports, like skiing and snowmobiling. Kids make snow forts and snowmen, and sled down powdered hills. We enjoy seeing the gorgeous waves of snow, especially when the rarely seen sun pops out—and everyone's mood seems to improve. We don't always like the discomfort of winter, but we do appreciate the season as part of our daily bread. Life happens in the winter, just as it does during the other seasons.

In the original shooting manuscript for the movie—much of which had to be deleted for the sake of the film's length—Shep referred to the "perpetual meat loaf" that was sizzling in the Parker oven. The meat loaf was indeed perpetual. It was *always* there. One could eternally count on a good, hearty meal at the family table. In short, the Parkers had their daily bread, worthy of appreciation. The Bumpus hounds could steal one special turkey, but not the Parkers' God-provided, Mom-made meat loaf.

In *A Christmas Story*, then, meat loaf is more than a routine meal. It represents sustenance for body, mind, and soul—a lesson that sometimes only common folks can appreciate, like a good cup of diner coffee. Amen?

## CHAPTER 15

# Take Time Out to Seek Refuge

In my conversations with Jean Shepherd, he loved to repeat this line: "Humor helps us recognize that we, too, have lived—and survived." But he always added that life will be difficult along the way. We all face hardships. As needed, we must take time out from the journey to seek refuge.

This is one of the most significant life lessons in *A Christmas Story*. If we don't sometimes retreat to our own sanctuary, our struggles can overwhelm us. We can lose hope in others and ourselves. We might become lonely, cynical people.

In the movie, Shepherd addresses the need for refuge through the story of Randy climbing into the cabinet under the kitchen sink. Randy is terribly distraught because he witnessed Ralphie pounding the day-lights out of Scut Farkus, the chief bully. He's also upset because he knows that Mom heard Ralphie madly spewing profanity and obscenity while beating up Scut.

In Randy's mind, the Old Man will have to punish Ralphie severely. Randy can't imagine a way out of the mess. He's overwhelmed, worried, and filled with concern for Ralphie. What will happen to Ralphie and the family? The forthcoming hour of likely doom is wearing on his heart. As Shep says, "The light was getting purple and soft outside. Almost time for my father to come home from work."

Mom hears Randy whimpering in his under-the-sink hiding place. She gently checks in on Randy, knowing he's deeply upset. She asks, "What's the matter? What are you crying for?" Randy responds, "Daddy's gonna kill Ralphie." She comforts Randy in his safe haven, telling him, "I promise you, Daddy is not going to kill Ralphie."

## Do We All Need Times and Places of Refuge?

Shepherd rarely talked about his personal-emotional struggles, but he had plenty of them. He could tell stories wonderfully, but he couldn't always manage his own, real-life story. He realized that when negative emotions overwhelm us, we tend to fear the worst. We play out scenarios in our minds, like minor nightmares. What if *this* occurs to us? What if *that* happens? How can we deal with the future, even the next hour? His usual coping mechanism was to get away from people—to seek refuge by himself. It was the only way he could prepare to reenter life so he could tell more stories.

Mom seeks to comfort Randy. She says to him, "Why don't you come on out of there?" With the various scenarios running through his mind, though, Randy is not ready for that courageous step back into the uncertain world. He still needs his place of refuge.

So, in one of the most wonderful scenes of motherly love in the movie, she gently touches Randy's cheek and then asks if he would like some milk. Randy can handle that small step out of his sanctuary. Milk, of course, is both a comforting kid food and a sign of maternal love. Mom gives him a glass of milk and says, "All right? See you later? Okay. Bye-bye." Mom closes the cabinet door, leaving it open just enough for Randy to have some light and for her to hear him.

In this scene, Mom signals to Randy that no matter what happens in the next few minutes, she will be there for him. She will remain his refuge when, eventually, he will have to leave the shelter of his cabinet hideaway—just as he will have to leave home one day.

Shepherd said that an early script had Randy hiding under the sink in the upstairs bathroom. But that was too distant from Mom, who is making dinner in the kitchen and watching for the Old Man's return home from work. In his kitchen refuge, Randy can hear Mom working and know that she's nearby. And Mom can better monitor him for any signs of deeper distress. She's comforted by the fact that Randy has agreed to see her "later." He's just not yet prepared to face the disquieting world. That's okay, for now. Our needed sanctuaries are always temporary.

Next, Shepherd masterfully—with Bob Clark's amazing direction—shows Ralphie retiring to his common place of refuge, his bedroom. Like Randy, Ralphie expects serious punishment for fighting and especially for his nonstop stream of swearing. He has already faced the Old Man's wrath for uttering the F-bomb while changing the car tire. This latest swearing episode will just rile up the Old Man even more. To Ralphie, there is no way out. And he knows that he can't stay in his bedroom retreat forever.

Ralphie lies in bed, weeping. Shep says, "I heard the car roar up the driveway, and a wave of terror broke over me. He will know what I said, the awful things that I've said." Ralphie is thinking about all of the punishments he might face, from the guillotine to Chinese water torture. Ralphie looks out the window, into the dark night, as his father rushes from the car to the door amid the Old Man's ever-present nemeses, the Bumpus hounds.

We know as viewers that a potentially dreadful scene is unfolding before our eyes. We feel Ralphie's tension, on the heels of witnessing Randy's distress. What will happen? Is there hope? If Ralphie were a bit older, it could be one of those scenes in which he would dream about running away from home, seeking refuge in a nearby wooded area, or sneaking off to a friend's house where he might hide for a while.

This is where Shepherd's life-affirming humor becomes a marvelous balm. Mom is not going to let anything more distressing happen to Randy or Ralphie.

Ralphie heads downstairs to face his fate like a man, fearful but consigned. He's in the open now, vulnerable. No bed. No pillow. No refuge.

The Parker clan gathers around the table for the nightly meal ritual as the Old Man reports he's "starving to death." His immediate concern is purely biological—relief from hunger. He has probably had his own rough day at work—which in many Shepherd stories is called the "g-d-d---ed office." This is Shepherd's reference to Adam being cursed to work in pain after humankind's fall from grace.

The Old Man is surprised to see Randy leave the cabinet, but he observes too many strange events in the Parker house to worry about this one; kids will be kids. "Well, what happened today?" asks the Old Man, innocently.

This is one of the greatest points of tension in the entire film. What will Mom say? Will Ralphie confess? What could possibly occur next? Can any hope emerge from this unfolding tragedy?

## Is the Old Man a "God" Figure?

In Shepherd's allegorical storytelling, the Old Man is like God after the fall from grace. Once Adam and Eve sin in the garden of Eden, God enters the scene and asks them where they are. God's question is not literally geographical; he knows where they are within the garden. God wants to know where they are at in their hearts, even their souls. It reminds me of a term that was popular in Chicago when I was a kid, "What's shakin'?" It meant, "What's going on with you—how are you really doing? Don't BS me." In his parables, Shepherd was always looking for the underlying meanings related to human nature, such as guilt, fear, and salvation. The Old Man is the magistrate—the God figure. His sons are the worried and sometimes guilt-feeling brothers.

Randy and Ralphie have to leave their hiding places and come into the open, before their highest judge, the Old Man. They realize that they are facing a seemingly no-win situation. Randy hasn't done anything wrong, but he can't help but fear for his brother; they are in it together since Randy was a witness to the fight and swearing, and any punishment will affect them both. What happens next will affect all family relationships, and potentially even set the course for the rest of the film.

In short, Mom saves Ralphie and thereby also comforts Randy. Mom reports to the Old Man that "nothing much" happened today;

Ralphie just "had a fight." She adds, "Oh you know how boys are. I gave him a talking-to." However, her previous words with Ralphie and Randy were words of comfort, not correction, and certainly not punishment. She knows that boys will be boys, and men will be men. They both need help—salvation, of sorts. She changes the subject, mentioning the upcoming Chicago Bears game in Green Bay.

What Mom actually does here is take on the burdens of Ralphie's guilt and Randy's fear. She will be responsible for what happened—at least before the face of the Old Man, who otherwise might dispense excessive justice. She's her sons' temporary refuge. She has probably been planning this family scene in her mind while preparing dinner. She knows what she needs to do. What she *must* do. She will ensure that if anything more goes wrong, the burden will fall on her strong shoulders, not on her sons' fragile hearts.

The scene then becomes a turning point in the movie and indeed in Ralphie's life. As Shep puts it, Ralphie "slowly began to realize that [he] was not about to be destroyed." Finally, Shep delivers one of the most amazing insights in the entire movie: "From then on, things were different between me and my mother." "Different," here, is one of the great understatements in *A Christmas Story*, a film loaded with hyperbole. Ralphie, as the eldest son, is being transformed by his mother's loving care. He realizes that *she* will always be his refuge.

Ralphie not only stops crying and ceases worrying about his fate. He begins eating his dinner, with relief and vigor. His mother has provided a personal sanctuary in his time of need. And she has signaled that she will forever be there for him, acting as his own, special island amid life's turbulent waters.

Randy is too young to understand this fully, but he nevertheless witnesses Mom's love. He should not fear coming out of his cabinet refuge again when the stakes seem high and his mind is dreaming up horrible scenarios. He imagined his dad "killing" Ralphie, figuratively speaking. But that will not happen now or in the future because of Mom's undying, sacrificial love for her children.

We humans can find refuge not just in places, but also in people—especially those who unconditionally love us. Ralphie and Randy discover this with their amazingly compassionate mother. Any mother-type figure in our lives helps us to stop our squirrely minds from playing and replaying troubling scenarios that are not likely to come to pass anyway. The future is rarely as bad as we can imagine, especially when we are protected under the wings of a nurturing parent.

When I was growing up in a highly dysfunctional home, I found nightly refuge in my bed. The feel of the sheets and covers as well as the smell of the flat, feathered pillow gave me a sense of safety, particularly when my parents were verbally and physically fighting in the tiny living room down the hall; I could hear it all, including words about killing each other. But my bed was there, every evening, night after night. And the same pillow. I can still remember the feel and smell of that raggedy pillow.

Of all of the scenes in *A Christmas Story*, I am most touched by three—when Mom comforts Randy in the cabinet, when the Old Man nonverbally expresses his delight as Ralphie unwraps and then loads his new Red Ryder rifle, and when Mom and the Old Man find comfort while sitting next to each other on the sofa on Christmas evening. All three scenes give me a sense of a home where there is refuge from the storms of life. As Shepherd said, humor helps us to know that we, too, have lived—and survived.

# CHAPTER 16

# Embrace Unexpected Delights

Jean Shepherd was known for inviting out for coffee the fans who stayed around after his one-man performances, and then regaling them with his tales. Of course, he appreciated the attention. But he also enjoyed delighting guests who never expected to be able to spend time with him personally.

One of the important life lessons in *A Christmas Story* is that we should embrace unexpected delights. When we live only according to our own, often excessive expectations, we might be let down. Resentments will grow in our hearts.

If we think we will be disappointed, we probably will be; our mindset significantly influences how we experience the future. But when we embrace the joy that comes with unforeseen adventures, we find that life has far more to offer us than we ever imagined. We just have to open our hearts and minds along the way.

I was leaving my Michigan campus office one brutally cold evening while the sun was setting. As the building door closed behind me, I glanced to the west and witnessed one of the most spectacular sunsets I had ever observed. Flashes of crimson broke through distant snow clouds, with green and yellow hues. I put my briefcase down on the ice and simply watched the unfolding beauty. It occurred to me that the scene I was watching would never be replicated, anywhere. Meanwhile, departing students were flying past me, cell phones in hand, running to their cars, wondering why in the world I was standing in the blustery cold air.

One of the scenes in *A Christmas Story* that people like to bring up in conversations with me about the film occurs near the end, after the disastrous fiasco with the Bumpus hounds stealing the golden-brown turkey off the Parkers' kitchen table.

The Old Man quickly resolves that the family will go out for dinner on Christmas Day. What else can they do? Leftover meat loaf wouldn't be acceptable for a special holiday meal. They can't suddenly invite themselves to the home of a neighbor, family friend, or relative. They are stuck, holding the turkey wing, so to speak—as the Old Man literally does, personally crushed by  what happened while he was peacefully enjoying the newspaper comics and imagining carving the turkey.

In the movie, the Old Man simply says, "All right! Everybody upstairs. Get dressed. We are going out to eat." But in the original shooting script, the Old Man declares, "Get your coats! We're going to the Chinese joint. We're going to have chop suey!"

I like the original wording because it suggests low expectations—chop suey versus roasted turkey! On the other hand, by not giving away where they are going to dine and what they might order, the film visually surprises the audience with the subsequent exterior shot of Bo Ling & Sons Chop Suey Palace. This is, after all, the only restaurant in town open on Christmas Day. The aesthetics are unimportant. If the restaurant is warm and serves hot food, the place is more than acceptable. It's Christmas!

## Why Go Out for Chinese Duck on Christmas?

The easy answer is that it was supposedly the only restaurant open on the holiday. But Shepherd wanted the Parker family to go somewhere atypical—even "exotic," in the sense that it would not have been part of their regular cultural habits. He wanted the family to experience something atypical, beyond the already-special treat of turkey on Christmas. At that time, there would not have been many "foreign-food" restaurants, and certainly none—like German or Italian—open on Christmas. The neon sign is "Bowling," but the letter "w" is not functioning (an intentional visual gag). The restaurant door says "Bo Ling & Sons Chop Suey Palace." A "palace"—how exotic! And the duck? The idea was to serve one bird as a substitute for another bird—duck for turkey. Quite visually unusual—and fun!

Sometimes the best scenes in movies are improvised. This happens at the Chinese restaurant. The script simply directed the waiter to carry to the table a tray "bearing a large duck." Then, the waiter would place the plate on the table and the family would "dig in." That was it. Shep just adds that the Christmas meal would live in the family's memories—and then on to the final scene of Ralphie and Randy in bed with their new gifts on Christmas night.

Ironically, the scene actually became a significant source of unexpected delight for the actors and eventual viewers. The waiter delivers the whole duck on a platter. But the duck's head proudly rises up in the air, pointing forward as if swimming on a tabletop stream. Unnerved by this unexpected presentation, the family laughs somewhat nervously, especially Mom and the kids. The duck's noodle looks rather comical—almost like it's alive.

As the actors playing Mom and the kids laugh at the comical-looking duck, the Old Man gestures, to the proprietor, his discomfort with the head, on behalf of the family (actor Darren McGavin knew the full duck was coming). The Old Man hopes the owner will fix the culinary presentation. After all, what would the Old Man himself do with the head? Eat it? No way! Take it home in a doggie bag, perhaps to feed to the Bumpus hounds along with some arsenic? The proprietor suddenly comprehends the issue, grabs a hidden meat cleaver, and—BAM!—instantly severs the head.

Not expecting any of this to happen, the actress playing Mom, Melinda Dillon, erupts in uncontrollable laughter during the scene. The camera is running. She is acting—or is she? Not really. She has been hit with unexpected delight. So have we. What could have been a solemn meal, a disappointing backup to the golden turkey, is suddenly a source of hilarity. It's a brilliant, partly unscripted scene that captures the spirit of human delight in unforeseen circumstances.

In fact, the whole restaurant episode conveys this life lesson of embracing unexpected delights. The restaurant sign is itself a source of humor—if you catch the broken neon light. The Asian servers singing holiday classics is probably politically incorrect by today's standards—as if the movie is intentionally making fun of the staff's difficulty in pronouncing some letters: "Fah rah, rah, rah, rah" instead of "Fa la la la la."

Yet, we can consider that singing from a positive angle. The restaurant owner wants to honor the Christmas holiday on behalf of his guests. He also desires to entertain if not delight them by performing the carols. He's appreciative for the only customers that he may have that Christmas Day. He's doing his best to make the meal and the entire restaurant visit as special as possible.

The owner first sings a Christmas song himself, with proper pronunciation. Then he cues his coworkers to sing on their own. But when he realizes that his staff can't quite use correct English pronunciation, he calls a halt to the singing—perhaps to avoid embarrassment both for the guests and his staff. In either case, it makes perfect sense for the Parker clan to accept the owner's hospitality by smiling with delight.

## Why Does the Old Man Say "Frah-JEE-lay"?

Of course, the package says "FRAGILE." But Shepherd wants to convey that the Old Man is truly a fake literary genius. The head of the Parker family indeed won a literary award—a *major* award. But can he pronounce a relatively common word correctly—especially in the excitement of unpacking his "baby"? Ironically, the literary expert mispronounces the word ("frah-JEE-lay"), suggesting maybe it's Italian. Besides, to him, Italian is exotic, in tune with the leg lamp itself. Maybe he knows Navajo as well, giving him a special connection to Red Ryder's companion, Little Beaver.

The award-unpacking scene is another source of unexpected delight. We wonder what the major award will be, especially given the enormous wooden crate. Clearly, it's not the bowling alley that the Old Man optimistically predicted. Nor is it a tiny item, like a wooden plaque or a chrome trophy. It's large and heavy enough to be packed in a sturdy wooden crate and wheeled into the living room on a dolly.

Then, the Old Man holds up the large plastic leg. What in the world? In his brilliance, the Old Man initially suggests it might be a statue. That would seem fitting for a literary award—although a statue of the head of the Lone Ranger's nephew's horse might be more fitting.

Of course, if it were just a leg statue, it would be of absolutely no practical use to the Old Man. It could have been a delightful gag gift—a great source of laughter for the Parker kin and visitors: "Look at the silly statue I won, probably designed by those dopes at the Art Institute in Chicago." That alone would have been an absurd delight. But the Old Man's pride is at stake; he's sure that there must be more to such a "major award" meant to honor a great mind like his.

As Mom holds the leg lamp close to her heart, the Old Man climbs out of the carton. The nutty leg statue appears to be a real, functioning lamp. The prize has utility apart from its apparent highbrow aesthetics. The Old Man has uncovered quite a buried treasure.

I have always been delighted by Shepherd's use of just the right but unanticipated words in his stories. He could work for hours or days to come up with the perfect word for a specific situation. Frequently, such key words point to the underlying meaning in his parables. When Mom holds up the leg lamp for the Old Man to view, the Old Man's eyes "boggled." One meaning of that word is "confused." Another meaning is "to be astonished or overwhelmed." Yet another meaning, describing his physical eyes, suggests they are "vibrating or bulging in and out." Shepherd uses this word because he's trying to convey all three things at once—the Old Man's confusion, astonishment, and sensual excitement.

Imagine how stunned Ralphie and Randy are with the unfolding scenario. Such a large prize is totally unexpected. This "thing"—whatever exactly it is and what it's for, besides shining light—is even kid-boggling. Ralphie gets it, somewhat, as he begins stroking the leg, much to the chagrin of Mom. He's not yet aware of it, but his male hormones are kicking in.

Most unexpected of all, however, is the strange power that the gift seems to hold over the Old Man. He's mesmerized. Hypnotized. Clearly the prize is more than he ever imagined because of the spell that it casts upon him. He is lost in the lamp's sway over his rationality. Art has swept him up in a kind of pride-shimmering bliss.

## Is the Old Man's Leg Lamp Truly a Serious Matter?

Shepherd told me that instead of merely laughing at the silliness of something, we can become far too serious about it—even irrational. In the Old Man's case, we wouldn't expect him to completely overcome his excitement and immediately toss the new lamp into the trash—although some award recipients might do so. A "normal" recipient might see it like receiving an ugly tie for Christmas that he knows he will never wear; why not just throw it out, give it to the local thrift shop, or place it on the Bumpuses' porch as a surprise gift—with a special, unsigned message: "A SCARF FOR ONE OF YOUR STINKIN' HOUNDS"? The Old Man can't possibly do anything like that with his major award. To him, the lamp is a deeply serious matter, a solemn honor that only a brilliant mind like his can fully fathom.

Both because of its erotic appearance and its capacity to produce glowing light, the leg lamp is a seductive item. It's a "thing" that works; it turns on. At that point, the Old Man can't see it just as a source of unexpected delight. His vanity overwhelms him; the leg lamp is his "major award," somehow connected via invisible electrons to his masculinity. Lacking any sense of amusement—only pride mixed with bizarre sensuality—he misses the opportunity to make unpacking the major award into one of the great tales of Parker-family humor. He has lost all sense of humility, and thus, of humor.

Seduced by forces beyond his control, the Old Man adopts the serious extreme, turning the leg lamp into a type of idol. He expects neighbors to use the image of the leg lamp as a medium for venerating his special, advanced intelligence—what the Old Man tells neighbor Swede is his contest-winning "mind power." As a result, neither the Old Man nor his family can simply enjoy the lamp as an unexpected, largely absurd prize. There will be no delight in the lamp unless something changes.

Imagine if the Parker clan were able to howl with laughter at the lamp during the unpacking. The Old Man could have said, "Hey, I thought I was getting fifty thousand dollars or maybe a bowling alley, not some silly piece of art. This cheap leg looks like it was caught with a fishing net in one of the smelly ponds over by the steel plant. I told you those literary-contest people are lug nuts. This rubbish is what I get for knowin' the Lone Ranger's nephew's stinkin' horse—whatever his name is. Forget it. I don't want to waste a fuse hooking it up. Come on, let's have supper. I'm hungry. The meat loaf smells great."

I could even imagine Ralphie and the Old Man setting up the leg lamp in the backyard for target practice on Christmas morning. Or simply putting it somewhere in the house where the Parker gang could periodically laugh together at the ridiculous prize—and show it with feigned excitement and plenty of delight to visitors. Today, the lamp might serve admirably as a gag item in a man cave. Or why not regift it to Aunt Clara? Imagine her receiving and unpacking it. It might fit her bunny-inspired decor perfectly.

In other words, life offers us a wide variety of unpredictable delights. We have opportunities to reimagine the meaning of unforeseen encumbrances. As Shepherd believed, if we can stay open to their arrival in our everyday lives, identify them, and not take them too flippantly *or* too seriously, we will be much happier people. Unfortunately, if something doesn't match our immediate expectations, we tend to discount it. Or worse, we turn it into a kind of idol of attention or pride.

My wife and I appreciate unexpected delights in our shared avocation of birding (bird watching). We have done it around the country, including near Shepherd's home on Sanibel Island. You never know what to expect during a birding adventure.

On one excursion, an uncommon Florida scrub-jay landed on my head and began pulling out my already-thinning hair. I didn't know what to do. While my wife howled with delight, I let the stinker pluck at my pate. When he finally took off, I put my hand on my head to assess the damage. Then I looked at my hand, which was smeared with a combination of bird poop and blood. I had been pricked and shat upon by a relatively rare species. What an unexpected delight!

Yet, we meet other birders who are so committed to adding additional species to their life list of bird sightings that they don't seem able to enjoy the time and place, like a quiet morning at a placid lake or in a verdant forest. Delightful yet unexpected vistas suddenly appear when we're hiking the birding trails. Similarly, other creatures show up—like the armadillo that hobbled between my legs while I was standing still with my binoculars to spot birds. We saw a mommy alligator protecting her twenty-one little babies. I had no desire to imitate the Old Man by sticking my foot near them for a nibble.

Shepherd aimed to create significant unpredictability in his stories, both because it's good drama and because that's the way life actually is—if we pay attention. Who could have even imagined that the

Bumpus hounds would snatch the turkey? Or that the Parker family would eat Christmas dinner at a chop suey "joint"? Or that the restaurant proprietor would chop off the duck's head in front of the family? Or that the Old Man's "major award" would be a life-size leg lamp that looked like a bordello accessory? Or that a rare Florida scrub-jay would do a number on my noggin?

## Why Do We Enjoy Rewatching A Christmas Story?

Most of us who watch *A Christmas Story* have already seen it—often multiple times. We know what will happen! We even enjoy the predictability. Why? Shepherd said that "participating" in a well-told story can be a meaningful ritual. The best stories lure us back repeatedly, so we can enjoy the same meanings and experiences. In Shepherd's view, this is what makes great storytelling like religious rituals. We want to repetitively experience the "good news" of the story.

Shepherd encourages us to keep open hearts and minds amid the routines of life. We just might discover new delights worth sharing as humorous stories. For some straitlaced adults, expecting delight can be quite a "fragile" state of mind. Get over it! Even humor directed at ourselves can be a delight to behold. Pass me some more plum sauce with the roasted duck—but without the upturned head, please.

## CHAPTER 17

# Join the Choir of Life

As the credits are running near the beginning of *A Christmas Story*, we see downtown Hohman, Indiana, preparing for the holiday. A Salvation Army brass band plays "Jingle Bells." A group of choristers belts out "Go Tell It on the Mountain" while circled around a warm fire on the blustery night.

As soon as I hear those and other songs in the movie's introduction, my heart lifts and I begin singing along—in my mind if not aloud. During the film's musical introduction, Shep says, "Downtown Hohman was prepared for its yearly bacchanalia of peace on earth and goodwill to men." Such holiday merriment calls for fitting music.

As in the film, our own Christmas season invites us to be jollier, to open our hearts to a time of grateful giving and receiving. Music helps us do so. It's a fitting beginning to the story of Ralphie and his family and friends. We can't imagine Christmas without recalling the season's music, both sacred and secular. Special times call for meaningful music that opens our hearts.

Here's an important life lesson in Shepherd's movie: Join the choir of life. Don't sit on the sideline or in the audience. And don't worry about whether or not you can carry a tune. Metaphorically and literally speaking, just start singing! Living with good cheer can itself be like singing. Each of our days can mirror the musical season of Christmas, when our hearts are full of gratitude and we reach out to one another with joy.

If you can sing in the shower or the car, you can sing your way through life. Your heart is open. If not, start now. Who cares what you sound like? Get your heart in the game of life. Even the mold in your shower is lonely without your song.

The Reformation's Martin Luther (1483–1546) reportedly said, "For if you want to revive the sad, startle the jovial, encourage the despairing, humble the conceited, pacify the raving, mollify the hate-filled . . . what can you find that is more efficacious than music?" He added that music captures the "emotions of the heart," urging people to virtues and vices. That's quite Shepherdesque.

One musical scene in *A Christmas Story* flies by so quickly that we might not catch its significance. And it's a real gas, as we used to say in the Windy City.

Having just purchased their annual Christmas tree at a prototypical outdoor lot, the Old Man and the rest of the Parker clan are heading home in victory. The Old Man is savoring the memory of bargaining successfully with the tree-lot peddler, who even tied the tree on the top of the piece-of-junk Olds for free. Such a deal!

## Why Did Shepherd Set Most of His Movies in Holidays?

Everything that occurs in our lives is part of the wondrous choral symphony of our days on earth. Every day can be more like the spirit of Christmas for each of us. But our days can also be more like Easter or Thanksgiving—even the Fourth of July. This is largely why Shepherd set most of his films in holidays, where the familiar music flows and the daily grind of life is interrupted with special meaning and purpose. During holidays, we rediscover what life most means for us.

The Old Man is driving, of course—he's a real man, in control of the car and everything else in life. He's on his game. The Old Man is steering the Parker sleigh toward home, over the river and through the woods—or at least through the dirty slush and into the spine-jarring potholes.

Nevertheless, we can tell that he's displeased. He seems to be irritated, looking like a curmudgeon. Why?

Because the rest of the family is singing "Jingle Bells" at the top of their lungs. He's not interested in such a slaphappy tune, sung by his kin or anyone else. That's kids' stuff, at best. It's silly racket in his ears and heart. He doesn't want to be in the family choir or the audience.

In spite of the Old Man's reluctance to join the vehicular choir, the song is wonderfully appropriate for singing together while riding in the family's sleigh—a 1937 Oldsmobile touring sedan. As the Old Man looks out the window and rolls his eyes, the rest of the Parkers belt out the lyrics. The killjoy behind the wheel has just proven his manly prowess at the tree lot and has no time for childishness. But the rest of the Parkers are a joyful, unified family.

Indeed, when the family reaches the end of the tune, practically shouting rather than singing "one horse open sleigh," the two brothers and Mom really let loose. In unison, like it was premeditated, they bellow a Bronx cheer—or, as we used to say in Chicago, they cut a healthy heap of "the raspberries."

## Why Are Farts Universally Funny?

Farts are a quasi-musical sound that kids absolutely love. Adults generally do as well, across cultures, even if they won't admit it. For one thing, such noisy gas is unpredictable. It just happens, often as a surprise attack on social propriety. People-produced, fart-like sounds are also a kind of universal language that Shepherd uses sparsely in his humor because they can become comedic gimmicks. The Bronx cheer and the like are the wonderfully unadulterated, unrefined, primordial imitations of the sound of a toot, fart, gas, buster, or whatever it was called in your childhood. In the movie, the raspberries become the song's coda, like an exclamation mark. The sound means only one, important thing: fun. To join this automobile choir is to participate in shared frivolity. The Parkers have jingled their gusty bells together—minus the Old Man. How can he not laugh at what just happened in his freezing Olds? Is he not a member of the human species? By the way, there is a kind of a professional artist, called a "flatulist," who specializes in fart performances. Such an artist masters a particular form of humor. Shepherd once did a radio show on this topic.

As Shepherd believed, life is not meant to be merely solemn or analytical. We humans are created for amusement as well as work. Enjoyment is in our genes. It's hard to imagine any other creatures bemusing themselves this way. It's simply a right and fitting human thing to do.

We just have to let our joy ring out, together. When we do, we join the choir of life, with its many melodies and near-harmonies. Humor and music are two ways that we can participate in the choir. When they're combined, it's hard to just sit silently in the audience like the Old Man.

That's the kind of heartwarming, life-affirming impact Shepherd wanted in *A Christmas Story*. The whole movie is like a choral production by the various characters, tied together by overlapping dreams, challenges, and humorous life experiences. Shep clues us in to the harmonies and disharmonies of Parker-family life, helping us sing together to remind ourselves that we are wondrously, gloriously, alive. "Jingle your bells!"

Shepherd wrote and told stories to help people experience the music of life even amid difficulties. Singing "Jingle Bells" together in the car might not seem like it can help us learn a significant life lesson. If so, we take ourselves a bit too seriously. Think again. Don't lose your joy in life because of your heart-numbing seriousness! Accept some self-created amusement.

Grave seriousness is one of the Old Man's heart-suffocating limitations in life. He holds back on unadulterated fun. He wants to get the Christmas tree home, set it up, decorate it, and most of all plug in the tree lights. He's technically inclined and results oriented, as Shepherd believed men tend to be. Give the Old Man a task; don't invite him to the party. He will just be a downer for everyone else.

So, in the car ride back home from buying the tree, he's probably imagining all of the wonderful work he's going to accomplish while setting up the tree. The Old Man is likely pondering the electrical circuits and power cords, lights and action, especially turning on the Christmas lights for the first time to impress the family with his excellent tree purchase, jazzed up by his superior expertise in household wiring. Just as Ralphie dreamed about the A+ "romance" with Miss Shields, the Old Man is daydreaming about the accolades he will receive in response to his magnificent Christmas-tree presentation. To him, the jovial singing is just a distraction.

## Who Is Riding in the Back Seat with Ralphie?

In the introduction, I mentioned that Shepherd and the movie's director, Bob Clark, wanted all viewers to experience Christmas through the childhood wonder of Ralphie. We are Ralphie, riding in the back seat of the Olds with his brother, and with Mom up front, singing along with unbridled joy. We can identify with the other characters as well, but Ralphie is meant to be the character who most delivers us to wonder and delight. That's his calling in the film. Ours is to ride along with him.

Because of the Old Man's curmudgeonly attitude, this short scene of singing "Jingle Bells" in the car is a wonderful illustration of our human need to join the choir of life. Shepherd believed women and kids have a natural knack for breaking into song, going with the flow of emerging delight, even just goofing around. They open their hearts to one another, coming together in song.

Men, on the other hand, tend to hold back. This is why the Old Man remains silent in his beloved—and hated—Olds. Singing "Jingle Bells" is beneath his self-important manliness. He thinks he needs such fun like he needs another go-round with the Bumpus hounds in the driveway.

Not surprisingly, the Old Man gets his solemn due—a tire blow-out. The same guy who was silent during the joyous singing and fake tooting shouts, "Blowout!" Now he has got a real challenge. Now life really means something! He can set his time limit and tackle that flat tire like a member of a pit crew at the Indianapolis 500. He can prove his masculinity and impress the family. The Old Man will demonstrate his mettle. In four minutes or less. Oh, what fun it is to replace a tire on a slush-spewing road during an Indiana winter!

## Is the Tire-Changing Scene Tragic?

We laugh at the tire-changing scene, but it's also tragic—even apart from the F-bomb. If the Old Man could have joined in singing "Jingle Bells," he might not have become so impatient with Ralphie while changing the tire. His annoyance at the family's singing probably contributed to his impatience with Ralphie. As father and son, they might instead have had some fun together, even joked self-critically about the whole scenario: "Ralphie, here's a life lesson for you that I never learned: You get what you pay for—tires included! I probably spend more money getting these baldies repaired than I would if I just bought better ones to begin with. I hate to admit it, but your old man is a classic cheapskate. I bet the Bumpuses' dilapidated pickup truck has a superior spare tire." Instead, Ralphie is yet again distant emotionally from his father, torn by guilt for losing the wheel hardware and perhaps even fearful about how he will disappoint the Old Man. Ironic, but also tragic. Mom had hoped for father-son bonding when she suggested that Ralphie help change the tire.

The earnest Ralphie, proud to be working on something with his father, ends up blurting out the F-bomb and getting into real trouble. Nothing like a three-tired broken sleigh contest to bring out the worst in the Old Man.

Let me take this problem of male seriousness one step further: What if the Old Man had been able to keep Ralphie's "adult" language a secret between the two of them—a kind of father-son bonding? Suppose Ralphie's father had said something like this, "Wow, you sound like me, Ralphie. Mom doesn't like it when I get frustrated and bellow the F-bomb. I won't tell Mom what happened. Cross my heart and hope to fix this tire in three more minutes, with your help finding the scattered parts." Then, when they got back into the car, the Old Man could have taken the lead to start the family singing "Jingle Bells" again.

In Shepherd's view, men generally view silliness as a feminine or at least a childish trait. The ironies abound, because boys are even more likely than girls to play around with silly fart sounds. But when it comes to everyday family fun—part of the joyful choir of life—men are not the ringleaders, according to Shepherd. They need help from the rest of family.

Men do have their own follies when they gather with other men, but sharing those even privately when wives or girlfriends are around is another matter. To put it differently, males sometimes sing their own tunes as a kind of in-group chorus. And they get uncomfortable, even embarrassed, when they joke around within earshot of women.

From Shepherd's perspective, much of the future of the world hinges on men being able to enjoy things lightheartedly. Today, they just don't want to join what they consider to be sappy choirs—figuratively speaking. Indeed, ask any church choir director: It's harder to recruit men, who worry about looking and perhaps sounding foolish. Get over it, guys!

Still, choral music is powerful. It grabs our hearts. Singing with others is even more potent. It affects both singers and listeners. It gives extra meaning to life. As Luther said, it can revive the sad. Singing won't replace the flat tire, but it sure could make the process more fun for Ralphie than trying to beat a pit-repair time record with a grumpy, impatient father.

By analogy, life is a chorus, begging us to join. Let's not just sing alone in the shower or the car. We can enjoy life together, one tune at a time, until we are unafraid of celebrating the joy of the Christmas spirit all year long.

In *A Christmas Story*, Shepherd aimed to create scenes that would grab all ages and both sexes. He also wanted to make silliness palatable, particularly to adult males. He hoped that even hardheaded men would get the message that fun is for the whole family. Curmudgeons beware: Don't take yourself so seriously. Life is not really a blowout. Life is a gas.

## CHAPTER 18

# Let Your Light Shine

The leg lamp is *the* icon for *A Christmas Story*. We see it pictured on many movie-related products. We can buy replicas in all sizes. It's on greeting cards—like the 3D card I just received from a neighbor who sees the full-size lamp in my kitchen window every Christmas.

I visited a new restaurant three weeks before Christmas. Near the front door was a glowing replica of the movie lamp. Everyone coming through the front door pointed and smiled. It was a hit. "It looks pretty frah-JEE-lay," chuckled one entering customer.

The Old Man was "overcome by art" when he first saw the astonishing lamp. And he knew "just the place for it," in the front window of the Parkers' home. He would proudly broadcast his "major award," which was "glorious" and "indescribably beautiful." The "indescribable" part is especially true; try to describe the lamp to someone who has never seen it.

Decades ago, I visited the home where Jean Shepherd grew up in northern Indiana. I wanted to get a sense of the scale of the homes on the street, to imagine what it would be like "turning on" that neighborhood with the leg lamp at night. Of course, Shepherd's family never really had a leg lamp, but the idea of imagining it in the front window of his actual childhood home intrigued me.

## Was the Old Man an Early Rapper?

The Old Man's recurring victory chant is, "I won"—eight times, nearly in a row. He sure did win. The official telegram proved it. While waiting for the contest award to arrive at the Parker home, he dances a jig in the living room, right in front of the window that will eventually broadcast the lamp's fleshy glow. Hopping around, he sings like a rapper, "Tonight, tonight is gonna be the night. Tonight, tonight, hot d--n tonight." Shepherd, the master raconteur, captures the lingo perfectly; the prize will be sensually "hot," and it will begin to d--n his marriage that night. What a rap!

While I was standing in the shadows in front of the tiny, dilapidated house, an Asian woman came out the front door to ask in broken English what I was doing. Good question! At least she didn't call the police on me. I figured it was going to be too difficult to explain. There was no way I could describe it or try to act it out. (Think about that!) I apologized for bothering her and departed. Some things don't translate well cross-culturally—maybe like "Jingle Bells" at a Chinese restaurant.

After Mom gets Randy to show how the piggies eat, the Parker clan hears the anticipated knock on the door. The major award has arrived! What will it be? A cashier's check for fifty thousand dollars? A certified letter with a legal claim to a bowling alley in Terre Haute? A set of encyclopedias that the Old Man can use to cheat on future newspaper contests, when Mom's not around to answer questions? A lifetime supply of presharpened #2 pencils with colorful erasers and inscribed, "Mr. Parker—A Major Award Winner"? The possibilities are endless.

The Old Man directs the delivery guys to place the "FRAGILE" crate exactly where he wants to unveil his once-in-a-lifetime trophy. He calls on Ralphie to fetch a crowbar and hammer; the Old Man can't imagine leaving the crate out of his sight for a second. As the Old Man begins removing the top of the crate, he says to Mom, "Honey, there could be anything in there." Again, a true observation. It could be anything and, relatively speaking, nothing much.

At first, he can't find the item buried in all of the packing material. Then, the Old Man says excitedly, "Oh, boy. Oh, boy, oh boy . . . Would you look at that?" The Parker family is looking, taking it in, visually and mentally. This is becoming such a great moment in the history of the nondescript Parker clan from unexceptional Hohman, Indiana. The Old Man is about to put his street and even his town on the list of historical places. Rand McNally maps will never be the same. Truly boggling.

Then, confusion. What is it? A leg? Perhaps a leg "statue." The Old Man's aesthetic sensibilities are being aroused. But clearly, it's nothing like anything he could have imagined.

## Why Did Shepherd Love the Word "Excelsior"—the Prize-Packing Material?

"Excelsior" was one of Shepherd's favorite words because it means two diametrically opposed (ironic) things. First, it refers to the worthless, straw-like material used for packing the major award. Second, it means "upward and onward," or just "ever onward." The word is used on the seal of the Empire State (New York). It is similarly used for tickets to the observation floor of the Empire State Building (the eighty-sixth-floor "Excelsior Pass"). From Shepherd's perspective, what we humans think of as impressive (a major award) might actually be worth very little.

Then the Old Man is truly "overcome," as Shep says: "Holy smoke, would you . . . ? Do you know what this is?" The Old Man is excitedly dumbfounded. Even with his deep artistic sensibilities, he couldn't have guessed: "This is a lamp. . . . Isn't that great? What a great lamp." Great?

There is skepticism in his voice. He's deeply overcome, but he doesn't really know what to make of it. A leg lamp? What in the world does he need one of those for? Such a far cry from a bowling alley.

Yet, being as brilliant as he is—after all, he won the contest—he instantly knows "just the place for it. Dead center in the front room window." It will look like a live leg emanating from the living room. Better than a floodlit Rudolph, the red-nosed reindeer. Brilliant!

Okay, I think we can accept the Old Man's imperfect sense of artistic taste. But placing the illuminated leg lamp in the front window? That seems to be over the top. What in the world is he thinking—if he's rational at all? Where's his contest-winning intellect now? Isn't he supposed to be filled with Victor-like horse sense?

Swede, a neighbor played by the film's director, Bob Clark, joins the Old Man across the street to behold the rising statuary glory. Swede asks old man Parker what it is. The Old Man, carefully evaluating the placement of his breathtaking work of art in the window, replies, "Don't bother me now, Swede. I'm busy." Indeed, he is. Expert art curators spend weeks deciding where to place and how to illuminate artwork in new gallery installations. By contrast, the Old Man can pull off a new installation in seconds—setting, height, lighting, everything. Impressive!

Yet, the Old Man is busy in another way—making a fool of himself and probably his entire family. He proclaims to the gathering neighbors that the extraordinary item is "a major award." But Swede, whose aesthetic sensibilities are not quite as refined, still offers a brilliant critique: "Shucks, I wouldn't have knowed that. It looks like a lamp." One person's art is another person's lamp. Sounds like the history of modern art in a nutshell. Swede is one dazzling critic.

Finally, the Old Man reveals his genius, which earned him the distinctive statuary in the first place: "Yeah, mind power, Swede, mind power." Shep explains that the lamp "was a symbol of the old man's victory." Indeed, it was. He had finally won something big and impressive, even colorful, a sizzling work of art. It's the perfect fusion of form and function, look and feel. The lamp is something he can display to the world as a sign of his matchless intellect as well as his elevated artistic taste. After all, how many people actually know—even via a spouse—that Victor was the name of the Lone Ranger's nephew's horse? According to Mom, just about everybody except the Old Man.

The Old Man's grave blunder was insisting that he put the lamp where everyone would see it, up and down Cleveland Street, neighbor and visitor alike, maybe even for the Bumpus hounds to howl at. His incredible mind power seems to lack common sense. Although, to be fair to the Old Man, some people, like him, might actually enjoy seeing the lamp in the window at night. Art can be subjective—even seemingly kitschy statues. Maybe he and Mom should prepare for people from unknown parts of the world to be parading by the Parker house at all times of night. Sell tickets, Old Man! Maybe you can bring in enough booty to buy a dilapidated bowling alley.

## Is the Leg Lamp the Old Man's "Trophy Wife"?

Here's a lowbrow question for this man of such grand mental power: Why not celebrate the major award a bit more privately? You could put it in the window just one night, for fun. I bet Mom would have agreed to that. Then he and Mom could have moved it to a more discreet location, such as an end table, where just the family might savor it. I don't think it would be fair to the Old Man to require him to relegate it to the sooty basement, next to the clinker-creating furnace. He needs to proclaim his amazing victory more openly, above ground, at least. Ironically, the prize ends up buried, anyway. As Shepherd told me, the leg lamp became the Old Man's trophy wife, which he had to show off to the world. He was unable to carry on his "affair" with discretion.

Wherever the leg lamp might have ended up in the house apart from the front window, however, I would have recommended that the Old Man relish the pride of victory. He should turn it on routinely when the sun is setting, bathing in its yellow-orange glow—perhaps to the tune of Tchaikovsky's love theme. It would be the first leggy mood lamp in history. Why not? He won it. Sure, it was probably just a raffle prize among thousands of correct submissions. So what? What else has he won—ever? What are his life's triumphs? He's still battling the Bumpus hounds, the furnace, and the Olds. He doesn't have enough electrical outlets to keep from blowing fuses. Let the poor guy celebrate this high point in his life.

As Shepherd told me, we all have our quirky victories worth celebrating. We might have some high school trophies or a wristwatch earned for years of employment. We might even own a craft item we painstakingly created or inexpensively purchased that brings us joy. Maybe it was a gift. Or perhaps we just happened to run across it, a special find, like an archaeological treasure unearthed at a dusty tourist trap.

Decades ago, my son bought me a full-size leg lamp at an antique shop in Boston. Every Thanksgiving, my wife and I place it in our home's front kitchen window until the New Year, when we also take down our plastic Christmas tree. After we moved into a condo with a homeowner's association (HOA), I feared that "turning on" the neighborhood could elicit complaints. I was reluctant to test the powers that be.

Girding my loins for battle—as they say in the Bible—I nonetheless added the lamp to our kitchen-window holiday cheer, shining it brightly, with the inside lights turned off for maximum street-side impact. Beautiful! I just had to run outside to witness the glorious display. The window faces the main street from about twelve feet above ground, overlooking the leafless winter landscape—quite a roost for such blazing artwork.

I couldn't sleep well the first night we left it glowing; I got up in the wee hours to turn it off. "What the heck was I doing?" I wondered to myself. "Was I smitten like the Old Man? Totally bonkers?"

But the next day compliments started rolling in via email: "Thanks for displaying the funny lamp. We love it!" The following night, a vehicle filled with gawkers stopped in front of our house. A guy got out, trudged through the snow and up to our kitchen window. He looked carefully at the lamp—maybe to verify what it was. Then he snapped a photo. I should have opened the window and asked him if his name was Swede.

Nowadays, if I forget to mount the illuminated prop in time for Christmas, we hear from disappointed neighbors: "Where's the lamp? Did your wife break it?"

Let's pass along Shepherd's life lesson to everyone we know: "Let your light shine!" If necessary, turn it on yourself. If others enjoy it, great! If not, so be it. Don't be a jerk, but go for it!

Let's celebrate our little victories in life, even unexpected triumphs or unusual finds that others might not appreciate as deeply as we do.

They say that pride precedes a fall. That certainly happened with the Old Man's leg lamp. But why not rejoice over good things in life that we're rightly proud of? Even little things.

I love it when I see parents or grandparents flying inflated balloons from their roadside mailboxes to proclaim a newborn child or a recent graduate. If I had more courage, I would toot my car horn every time I drive by one of those "lamps." The folks are letting their light shine.

But, of course, let's not go over the top. One piece of art—or one award—"does not great relationships make"—to put it in highfalutin, Shakespearean language. Consider how others will react. Avoid the kind of "epic struggle" that grew between Mom and the Old Man. Don't honk your horn so loudly that you wake up the hounds and keep your neighbors up at night.

Some people will probably think your "major award" is magnificent. Great!

Someone else might think you're a weirdo. To quote what the Old Man says about Swede, your critic is probably just a "nincompoop." At least you'll feel better by thinking so.

Meanwhile, I will keep lighting up my leg lamp every Christmas. Until the HOA shuts me down. There is a fragile-minded Scrooge on every HOA board.

# CHAPTER 19

# Be a Hero

When I speak publicly about life lessons in *A Christmas Story*, I like to focus on one of the most intriguing aspects of Jean Shepherd's vision: Mom is a real, everyday hero, probably *the* hero in the movie and throughout Shepherd's voluminous stories. We can learn about how to be an everyday hero by observing her amazing actions as well as her capacious heart.

In the film, Ralphie and his buddies spar over whether or not a person's tongue would stick to frozen metal. As I mentioned earlier, Schwartz claims that his old man saw a guy stick his tongue to an icy railroad track, and that the fire department had to remove his tongue from the steel. Ralphie says he thinks that Schwartz is right.

In the shooting script for the film, Flick then pipes up, "Aw, jeez, you guys are real suckers for anything. My brother says that's an old wives' tale, and so does my mother." Schwartz replies, "Yeah, well, she's an Ol' Wife all right. She oughta know." Ralphie and Schwartz then offer what Shep calls "crazy kid laughter."

Also in the unused part of the script, Flick chimes in with an amazing response that helps us understand much more about the relationships between these boys and their respective mothers. Flick says, "Hey, watch it, Jerk-head. Don't talk about my ma!"

This is not just a way for Flick to counter the "Ol' Wife's Tale" slight. Shep explains: "Any reference to one's mother was like throwing down the gauntlet, no matter how vague or remote the slight. Just the mere mention of one's mother with any adjective in the dictionary, no matter how innocuous, was grounds for instant and ruinous vendetta."

Ralphie quickly jumps in to soften Schwartz's rhetoric: "Aw, he didn't mean nothin', Flick." Schwartz, the offender, follows up, "Yeah, you know I wouldn't say nothin' against your mother, Flick. I was just kidding." Finally, Flick moves beyond the conflict: "Yeah, well, just watch it." Then there is some arm punching, and everything is resolved, according to Shep.

Remember that Mom saves Ralphie from excessive punishment for his misdeeds. After Ralphie beats up the bully, Scut Farkus, Mom steps in to protect Ralphie from the Old Man's expected wrath. Ralphie and Randy both fear how the Old Man will react when he arrives home from work. Mom knows this. She comforts Randy in his refuge under the kitchen sink, tenderly touching his cheek and giving him a glass of milk. She safely keeps Ralphie's eyeglasses in her apron pocket after Randy finds them in the snow during Ralphie's fight with Scut. When the time is right, she slips the eyeglasses to Ralphie at the dinner table, preventing the Old Man's potential wrath.

## Why the Reverence for Mothers in the Movie?

Mom has a special place in *A Christmas Story*. There is no equivalent devotion for fathers in the shooting script, the final movie, or even throughout the corpus of Shepherd's storytelling. Dads do some wonderful things—like the Old Man buying Ralphie the Red Ryder BB rifle—but moms are always there, supporting their children, keeping the household going amid recurring chaos, often caused by their husbands as well as kids. Mom is the unsung hero in the movie, as was the case in Shepherd's own life.

Mom goes even further in that tense scene. Speaking to the Old Man, she minimizes the extent of the fight, "Oh, you know how boys are." She even fibs to the Old Man about giving Ralphie a verbal correction: "I gave him a talking-to." Yes, she comforted Ralphie! Randy and Ralphie are so relieved by their mother's words and deeds that they can now eat dinner in peace. Mom has served them admirably as the day's hero in their stressful lives.

Moreover, Mom never complains about her family tasks. She simply does what she must do to keep the household going. Shep exaggerates a claim in order to make a wonderful point about her service: Mom hadn't had a hot meal for herself in fifteen years. As the boys traverse the ground between home and school, Mom shuffles back and forth among a wringer washer, the stove, and the kitchen table. Except when cleaning the rest of the house or watering "the plant," she seems to live in that kitchen space.

We could say that the Old Man and Ralphie—perhaps even Randy—should be doing their part out of respect for Mom as a selfless person. But given the period portrayed in the movie, approximately 1940, such gender equality was not a major topic for discussion. Today, some might say that Mom was used as a doormat.

Mom simply did what was expected of her, often serving without regard for her own, personal needs. Perhaps we could say that being such a faithful mother was her vision of the good life for her and her whole family. In her view, she served as expected, considering her service a life calling.

Recall, too, that Mom as hero has to save the Old Man from his unbridled leg-lamp obsession. No one else can keep him under reasonable control—certainly not the children or the neighbors staring at the lamp in the Parkers' front window every night. The Old Man's overbaked pride for winning such a tough contest has gripped his soul. Mom knows it; she witnesses the smugness in the Old Man's actions, and chuckles to herself that he truly has lost his mind. He's loony! Mom is not. She brings reason to the Parker family.

The Old Man won't negotiate about where to place the illuminated leg in the house. He doesn't even want to turn off the lamp when the family leaves for a while, such as for Christmas-tree shopping. She has to take decisive action on behalf of the Parker clan. She courageously undermines the Old Man's undying infatuation by breaking the plastic lamp. What a gutsy hero! She did what was necessary; there was no other solution to the problem. The Old Man was intractably obsessed.

According to Shepherd, Mom is no dummy. She didn't like the Old Man's idea of getting the rifle for Ralphie in the first place, but she understands that she must comfort Ralphie in his distress after he gets hit with the BB. Moreover, Mom, as everyday hero, sees that telling the Old Man about the BB ricochet wouldn't help matters. She's going to protect her husband, too, from thinking that he made the wrong decision about purchasing the rifle for Ralphie. The Old Man did what he did; now Mom needs to do what she believes a loving mother and wife must do. She sees this kind of heroism as her purpose in life.

Ralphie often appreciates Mom's heroic actions. And he truly cares about her. He's old enough to begin to understand family dynamics and empathize with his parents.

After the Bumpus hounds snatch the turkey, the family gathers in the kitchen. Mom and Ralphie come down the stairs from the bathroom, where Mom has sympathetically tended to her oldest son's physical and emotional wounds. Mom witnesses the chaos left behind, tiny pieces of turkey and globs of gravy strewn across the table and around the checkered floor. The roasting pan is empty. Her labor was in vain. She breaks into tears.

Ralphie, in response, gives his mom the very washcloth that she has just used to comfort him. She uses it like a giant tissue to wipe away her tears. Ralphie and Mom truly love each other; she's his hero, who needs comfort in her own time of grief. Ralphie is her first beloved son, who will always care for her.

If the Old Man is the alleged family enforcer, Mom is the actual but sometimes subtle persuader. She influences partly by being a soothing role model for the children, even somewhat by being childlike herself. Mom is willing to stoop down to the level of a mama pig, encouraging Randy to eat like one. She can imagine herself as a frightened child hiding under the kitchen sink, and lets Randy stay in his sanctuary. In many ways, Mom humbles herself to serve others. She's not as much a suffering servant as an empathically infectious one. It's hard not to like, appreciate, and even love Mom.

Of course, we all grow up with family challenges. Just after I was born, my mother contracted tuberculosis and was confined to a sanitarium for most of the first year of my life. During that time, she also became schizophrenic—perhaps related to her postpartum depression and being separated from me and the rest of her family. She never was well again.

## Is Melinda Dillon's Portrayal of Mom Too Smart and Sexy?

One of the criticisms of the movie that Shepherd heard repeatedly was that the character of Mom seemed too smart and sexy. By contrast, Shepherd felt that Dillon really nailed the part, depicting Mom as smart, self-confident, self-respecting, and modest but attractive. I recall that, not long after the movie came out, I was at a public presentation with Shepherd. An attendee questioned the casting and portrayal of Mom. Shepherd got visibly angry. He shot back, "Well, then make your own d--- movie!" I couldn't help but think that Shepherd's defensiveness was akin to that offered by Ralphie and his friends when one of them would criticize someone else's mother. Moreover, it seemed to me Shepherd felt like the question was implicit criticism of his own mother.

As a result, she was not a nurturing mother. Worse yet, she was frequently combative. I never saw her as a hero—at best as a truculent survivor. But I did witness the amazing nurturing by my friends' mothers—and sometimes by their fathers as well. Each of our life stories is different, peppered with special challenges that can make it difficult for adults to be everyday heroes.

Nevertheless, I don't want to minimize Mom's everyday good works in *A Christmas Story*. Her ongoing actions and sentiments in the film suggest quite a tale of familial heroism. You might even try watching the movie with Mom in mind, paying attention not just to *what* she says, but also to *how* she says it. And monitor her facial expressions. I agree with Shepherd that Melinda Dillon was a great choice for playing Mom.

Mom is a subtly heroic parent who stays true to her immediate station in life. We can learn, from her life, a lesson for all of us, regardless of our own domestic situations, parents or grandparents. Clearly, Shepherd's mother had a positive impact on his life. In turn, Ralphie and Randy are being nurtured wisely and well by a caring mother.

Is there any redeeming hope for the Old Man as a hero in *A Christmas Story*? Yes!

He's not as likable as Mom; he can be abrupt, grumpy, and uninterested, often when he should be engaged with the family. I still get miffed thinking about him not singing "Jingle Bells" with his family as they rode their four-wheel sleigh home from Christmas-tree shopping. Lighten up, guy!

Yet—and this is a big "yet"—he's the one who buys the BB rifle and places it secretly for Ralphie to discover after Ralphie's initial disappointment on Christmas morning.

In one of the most moving scenes of the entire film, we witness the Old Man in his own childlike state of Christmas delight. He tears up as he sees Ralphie unwrap the rifle. His own excitement overcomes him as he demonstrates for Ralphie how to load the weapon and prepare it for use—even though Ralphie already knows how to do it. In short, the Old Man acts like a true hero, an empathetic father who wants the best for his son, as he remembers his own childhood pleasure and pride over his rifle.

In that remarkable scene with the Old Man and Ralphie exchanging endearing smiles, Mom clearly understands the males around her. In her own heroic way, she goes along with the rifle gift. Would she have agreed if the Old Man had first asked her about buying the rifle for Ralphie? Maybe not. But she could probably be persuaded because of her love as both wife and mother.

Even more importantly, she would be there for Ralphie either way. She would have detected Ralphie's disappointment and consoled him as perhaps only a truly heroic mother can. Thanks, Mom! And Melinda!

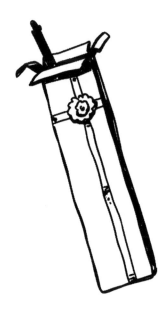

## CHAPTER 20

## Give Thanks

Let's begin this final chapter with thanks: Ralphie received his dream Christmas gift. The Old Man bought Ralphie the official Red Ryder carbine-action, 200-shot range model air rifle. We knew that Ralphie would somehow get one, but the joy for us is that it happened in an unexpected way—no thanks to the red-nosed Santa and his squirrely elves.

The look on Ralphie's face as he unwraps that special gift is priceless. He's beaming with delight, head to toe. Also, we get a sense from the glee on the Old Man's face that he's thankful he could surprise his son with the gift of his dreams. Two grateful guys—a giddy father and an ecstatic son—mirroring each other's appreciativeness.

What a festive scene! *A Christmas Story* could have ended right there, and we viewers would be grateful for a fine cinematic tribute to the Christmas spirit.

But consider what Ralphie had to go through to get to that glorious gift on Christmas morning. If only each of our lives was filled with clear reasons for gratitude all year long, without so many trials and disappointments! Getting to thankfulness is not always easy.

As we all know, the truth is that not all of our dreams will come true in life. Moreover, we will still have to face many frustrations while carrying on with our seemingly thankless routines.

The Old Man will probably battle the furnace for the rest of his earthly existence. It has become one of his unappreciated life callings. On the other hand, he seems to enjoy the battle. Perhaps it gives him *some* purpose in life—keeping the family warm by battling the cellar beast?

Randy will likely refuse to eat meat loaf now and again until he grows up and appreciates his daily bread more deeply. Mom's clever piggy persuasion will save the day for only so long. Yet, the family does have its "daily bread," even when Randy is ornery. As Mom says, not all people have food on their tables.

Ralphie will probably receive additional mediocre grades in school no matter how many times he daydreams about pleasing the teacher to the tune of Tchaikovsky's love theme. Still, do academic grades predict life success? I think not. Teachers and students are gifts to one another for many reasons beyond grades. I was a mediocre student and I've had many of them in my classes. But academic grades alone aren't the key to flourishing in life. Things like ethics and courage are also important. Ralphie displays them. My best teachers were role models for life, not just instructors. They encouraged me personally as well as academically. In fact, they showed me how to teach compassionately and influenced my decision to become a professor.

## Was the "Real" Ralphie a Good Student?

Shepherd based the character of Ralphie partly on himself as a child. Shepherd received mediocre grades up through college before dropping out. He even got a C+ in his college-level English writing course. Many years later, the same university gave him an honorary doctor of letters degree. Interestingly, the shooting script had Ralphie getting a C- from Miss Shields, but it was changed to the actual grade Shepherd received in his own college writing class.

The bullies will probably continue traversing the neighborhood, looking for vulnerable victims. Ralphie and his buddies might still have to avoid Scut Farkus and Grover Dill, along with any toady recruits to their foul gang. But along with life experience comes wisdom about how to deal with the bullies in our lives. Even just learning to avoid them is a gift. I give thanks that as much pain as they inflict on others, they are just as self-destructive; and there is space for their redemption.

The Old Man probably won't use better-quality spare tires for his Olds. After all, he mostly cares about trying to beat his four-minute tire-changing record. Even when the Indiana winter splashes waves of slush over his shoes and he loses wheel hardware because of his own impatience. In a sense, he's blessed by opportunities to pretend he's in the pits at the Indianapolis 500. Imagination is a gift. As are good dreams. Yet, I hope he's blessed with enough good sense to use tires with actual tread.

The Old Man will also continue to struggle with too many electrical cords and too few outlets—a burdensome law of supply and demand in the Parker household. He will have to keep buying packs of fuses to change like a bunny, hopping to the electrical box. Yet he gets satisfaction out of loading up the outlets and making the devices work. It's another entertaining challenge for him, even though it won't garner him any major awards. I just hope he keeps his home fire insurance up-to-date.

The Bumpus bloodhounds are likely to grow in number. I doubt that the Bumpus clan will get their dogs fixed. And, of course, the beasts will still try to ingratiate themselves to their favorite person in the world—the Old Man. It's not possible that the Old Man will ever take a liking to them since they snatched his golden turkey. Never again will he graciously let them nibble on his foot out the back door. Unrequited love is a sad situation in life. But maybe he will catch one of their ears in the door again! Surely that would give him some pleasure.

My point is that wonderful things happen to the Parkers and to us now and again, even when we see only the immediate challenges. Humor—humility—can be a wonderful response that fuels our gratitude for even little things, including the seemingly minor victories in life.

One of Jean Shepherd's most important lessons in *A Christmas Story* is that we should give thanks for each blessing—the great and small ones. Another way to put it is that grace—unexpected and often unmerited goodness—happens. And our natural response should be to offer thanks. When we thank others, we, too, are blessed. Expressions of gratitude are like our emotional daily bread. Even the small things in life, which we take most for granted, are worth celebrating.

This life lesson about giving thanks deepens the seminostalgic aspects of *A Christmas Story*. We all look back on our lives, not primarily because we would like to return to every one of "the good old days," but because we can see how we managed through challenging times and delighted in wonderful ones. We give thanks that we are still alive, that we are blessed with family and friends, that we avoided small and major disasters, and so much more.

Ralphie wakes up on Christmas morning, goes to the bedroom window, and surveys a winter wonderland of rolling waves of white snow and flashes of sparkling ice. He says, "Wow. Wow." Director Clark holds that shot to let it sink into our hearts. What a glorious morning! Why doesn't Ralphie just fly downstairs to see what's under the tree? Because the beautiful scene outdoors is itself a Christmas present to Ralphie and to us.

Finally, Ralphie wakes up Randy to dart downstairs together, where they begin sharing the annual joy of Christmas morning. Ralphie could have let Randy sleep so Ralphie could rummage through the presents in search of his rifle, without Randy being in the way. No, this is a morning meant for the gift of siblings as well as for packages under the tree—the tree for which the Old Man negotiated at the lot; the tree that nearly fell over when the Old Man tried to fix the star on top; the tree whose lighting challenged the Old Man's finesse with electrical cords. All is well!

Ralphie and Randy jockey for positions amid all of the presents. "Fire truck!" Randy declares, adding, "Oh boy, that's mine!" Ralphie looks desperately for his rifle, his disappointment mounting.

Mom and Dad come downstairs as well, still sleepy. It's time for the parents to enjoy seeing their jubilant children open gifts. Randy wants to be Santa, but he played that role last year. Ralphie is appointed the task, but is clearly disheartened by not seeing a package that looks like it could be a Red Ryder rifle. He will not be able to hold the one gift he most wants, the one he pitched to Mom, Miss Shields, and even desperately to Santa on the mountaintop. He won't have a chance to shoot at neighborhood villains, like Black Bart, to find his battlefield location with the compass in the stock, and to practice loading up his baby with packs of precious BBs. Bart and his devilish compadres will triumph on Cleveland Street.

But Christmas has arrived—and with it, Ralphie's annual gift from Aunt Clara, who still envisions Ralphie as a four-year-old girl. This time the present is totally embarrassing. What a low point, from hoping for the glorious rifle to receiving a ridiculous pair of pink bunny pajamas. Ralphie can't fight Bart and other baddies while wearing a silly bunny outfit made for a girl. He and the Old Man are not happy about Clara's gift, which the Old Man says makes Ralphie look like "a deranged Easter Bunny"—Darren McGavin's wonderfully ad-libbed line.

But Mom is still grateful for Aunt Clara's thoughtfulness, however misguided. "Isn't that sweet?" she says of the bunny outfit. She even calls it "the most precious thing I've ever seen in my life." Of course, she's merely honoring her sister's intention and hard work. Mom probably will send Clara a gracious thank-you note for the gift—and rightly so; it took considerable effort to make. Clara was thoughtful, if misguided. We all give thanks if we consider the good intents behind presents rather than just the gifts themselves.

Randy plays with his new zeppelin. The Old Man unwraps his can of Simoniz car wax. His Olds will still freeze up like a "g-d-d---ed pile of junk," but at least it will be a shiny heap of trash as it bounces through the Indiana potholes. The neighbors might be impressed, except probably for the Bumpuses.

Mom takes her turn distributing gifts. The Old Man gets his "blue" bowling ball, dumped on his lap. "Do you like it?" asks Mom. The Old Man responds, "Yes, very much. Very much." It's hard not to catch the double

meaning. The Old Man has more than a mere bowling ball to give thanks for.

All the gifts are opened—except for one missing present.

"Hey, that's funny," says the Old Man. "What's that over there behind the desk?"

"Where?" says Ralphie, looking around.

"Over behind the desk against the wall over there. Why don't you go check it out?"

Even Mom is caught off guard. Grace often enters our lives that way, seemingly out of the blue. How could this be? The Old Man is the only one that Ralphie didn't try to convince to buy the rifle.

Ralphie and his dad are delighted, son and father emotionally attuned to each other. It's the only time in the movie that this happens, although it's lightly foreshadowed early in the film when the Old Man suggests that Ralphie buy him a new furnace for Christmas. That can't happen, of course, but it's a joke that father and son can enjoy together. The Old Man dreams of winning the fight with the furnace. Ralphie imagines himself battling Black Bart rather than dark soot. But as the Old Man demonstrates how to pour BBs into the rifle chamber on this Christmas morning, he and Ralphie are filled with the joy of giving thanks together, for each other as well as for the rifle.

If only life were always bursting with such glad tidings!

Soon, the Bumpus hounds attack as the Old Man enjoys his newspaper comics. Disaster in the midst of grace. Anger and disbelief overtake gratitude.

Still, they celebrate Christmas together, eating duck at Bo Ling & Sons Chop Suey Palace. There is a reason to give thanks for that unexpected "daily bread" too. The family will have the joy of telling and retelling the story of the time they ate "chopped" duck on Christmas.

Eventually the kids get to bed, dreaming of their new toys. They are content. At peace. "Silent Night" plays in the background.

Finally, Shepherd and Clark deliver us an unexpected gift in the Parker parlor.

As "Silent Night" plays, Mom turns off the light. She says, "Oh, honey, come over here. Look at this." She and the Old Man sit next to each other, facing the very window where they battled over the leg lamp, next to the lit tree with its crooked star. Snow is falling, gently, peacefully, beautifully. They lift their wine glasses as a sign of peace, even as a declaration of gratitude for one another. The fight over that tawdry leg lamp has been resolved. Who cares now about the stolen turkey? The furnace is not clinking. Ralphie and Randy got the toys of their dreams. The Old Man places his arm on Mom's back and gently touches her neck; she slides her arm around his shoulder. "All is calm . . ."

Gratitude is the secret balm in our broken world. It comes to those who invite it into their longing hearts by acknowledging that all good things are gifts. Gratitude gobbles up our cynicism and criticism. If only we could create thankfulness on command, like wizards of good cheer! But gratitude, too, is a gift. Grace. After we seek gratitude and find it, we realize it was pursuing us all along. We just needed the heart to see and accept it. Somehow, it arrived.

We all are especially blessed by people who are gifts to us. My wife and children are gifts. Given my troubled childhood, I was likely destined to fall on my face as a husband and father, resentful of life's clinkers. I have fallen sometimes, but not completely. Neither my grandson nor I shot an eye out with my BB rifle. Neither did Shepherd, who grew up with his own, considerable challenges. There's hope!

Now I am blessed with two grandchildren. I experience the joy of childhood through them, like I did with my own offspring. Second and third chances in life are special gifts—do-overs from not quite getting it right the first time. I realize how insightful Shepherd was: We all are like Ralphie, kids at heart. I still eat my yogurt with my finger, right out of the carton—especially the vestiges that I can't get with a spoon. I keep dreaming forward in life.

And my wife steadies me, daily. She's the hero who puts up with me when I'm difficult to live with, fixated on my own leg-lamp-like obsessions. She admonishes me as needed. Sometimes I'm humble enough to accept her loving corrections. Now, I anticipate grace as part of the story of our marriage. And she lets me display our leg lamp in the window every year. She encourages me: "Let your light shine, old man!" She humors me.

Shepherd's final life lesson is the greatest one of all: Give thanks. Grace is our major award in the movie and in life. "All is bright . . ."

**Purchase signed copies of the book, dedicated personally to your friends and family, using the QR Code, above, or this address online: https://quentin-schultze.square.site/**

# Appendix

*You, Too, Have Lived—and Survived!*

## How to Create and Tell a
## Humorous Story like Jean Shepherd

Throughout this book, I have told humorous personal stories using the techniques I learned from Jean Shepherd, who wrote the screenplay for *A Christmas Story* and the stories that the movie is based on. In this appendix, I would like to share a seven-step storytelling process with you. These are my interpretations of Shepherd's process; I aim to be as faithful as possible to what he taught me.

Shepherd described his overall storytelling goal as helping the audience feel the following:

"You, too, have lived—and survived!"

### Step One: Identify "something" interesting that happened in your life.

It could involve a *thing* (a car, rifle, or leg lamp), an *event* (you just received a "major award"), a *person* (e.g., yourself, your spouse, a roommate, or a coworker), a *dream* (shooting a bad guy or getting an A+ on a school paper), an *idea*, and so forth. What happened in your life that grabbed your attention or imagination? The occurrence doesn't have to be anything "big." Keep tabs on the little things that are just part of life, like dealing with technology or the weather—dressing kids for school in the winter. According to Shepherd, you are hunting for even the seemingly minor "drama" in life that others can identify with.

### Step Two: Identify the parts of the story that involve "drama" and "character" (the latter could be called "personality" and might be a thing or a person).

Even everyday drama includes conflict—something that must be resolved. The "personality" is the person and/or "thing" involved—the "actors" in the story who contribute to the conflict. A furnace, car, or leg lamp could be a "personality." Imagine an event in your life that has interesting drama and characters, like going out to eat at a Chinese restaurant on Christmas or trying to get your young child to eat dinner.

### Step Three: Identify the compassionate humor in your unfolding tale.

"Compassionate humor" (my term) refers to something in a story that is inherently funny because we see it in *ourselves*—not because it ridicules *others*. As I indicated throughout the book, Shepherd's humor involves stories designed to help us see ourselves as we truly are. In various ways, we are like Mom, the Old Man, Ralphie, Randy, the bully, and others. There is even a bit of the Bumpuses in each of us.

Here's a great clue about identifying the compassionate humor in our everyday stories: Find the *irony*—the gap between what the characters are saying/believing, on the one hand, and actually doing, on the other. The Old Man says he is a "great mind." Really? We know that he got the answer to the newspaper contest from Mom! Yet we don't hold that against him; it is not a horrific character flaw. We love him even though he is a curmudgeonly character who thinks more highly of himself than he should. Don't we all?

## Step Four: Relate the humor to an emerging theme.

What's the point of the story—the message or theme? What's the life lesson—such as the lesson in each chapter of this book?

You don't have to say in your story what your theme is. In fact, you want the story itself to communicate the theme by the way you tell it. Shepherd did not have to say that Ralphie and the Old Man were great dreamers, and that we should pursue our dreams. Or that we can become obsessed with our dreams. Or that we should give thanks for wonderful things that happen in our life. Or that we should be flexible when life does not go the way we expect.

Shepherd believed that once you identify the theme of your story, you can tell it far more coherently. Once we recognize that the "bad" neighbors are "hillbillies," we can describe the Bumpuses as challenging neighbors. They are a bit uncouth, uncivilized. We don't want to be Bumpus-like neighbors—do we? The theme helps us determine what to say and how to say it.

## Step Five: Identify the points for exaggeration (or hyperbole).

In Shepherd's view, most compassionate humor works well when the storyteller exaggerates (or accentuates) aspects of the story—the drama or the personality, or both—and *sometimes* even the theme.

Here's why: Exaggeration helps us *better* capture the humor—and the *truth*—within a story. The Bumpuses did not own 785 hound dogs. But it seemed like it to the Old Man. The Olds did not freeze up all the time, but it seemed like it to the Old Man. The Old Man is so in love with his trophy wife (the leg lamp) that he wants to show it off exactly in the middle of the front window—like an art curator. It was not enough just to put it in the window!

## Step Six: Tell the story using only theme-relevant information.

Much of the hard work in compassionate humor is eliminating irrelevant aspects of the story. Like the best comedians, the best humorists whittle down the tale to just the essentials, within the existing time (if speaking) or space (if writing) limits.

What is essential to telling the audience about the leg lamp—maybe its sexy glow? Or about Randy's snowsuit (a tick about to pop)? Often only one or two key phrases or metaphors are sufficient. Randy says, "I hate meat loaf!" What else do we need to know about his feelings for the dinner fare? We can add a bit of exaggeration: "Beetloaf."

## Step Seven: Pay special attention to how you begin and end a humorous tale.

Think of the beginning of a story as immediately setting the scene—where, when, why, and who. Add something about how you felt: "I was trying to get the family in the car late one snowy night. I didn't want to miss all of the good Christmas trees!"

And think of the ending of the story as a line that provides a sense of closure: "Ralphie went back out to the world—wiser." Nothing like a crummy commercial to make one wiser about the media!

# About the Author

Quentin Schultze grew up in the shadows of Chicago's O'Hare Airport, dodging early jets that came in for landings over his childhood playing fields. When he was 16, his car was nearly crushed by an incoming aircraft as he took a shortcut across runways to deliver pizzas.

Inescapably, he became a fan of the Chicago Cubs, whose ever-frustrated team members taught him that life requires both skill and patience. His Windy City friends say that the Cubs, who repeatedly started each season strong and then nosedived after the mid-season break, turned him into a Calvinist. When the Cubs did win, it was usually the result of the opposing team's ineptness, not the Cubs' own crackerjacks.

"Quin," as his pals called him, was a demonstrably lousy student, barely graduating from the very high school that decades later gave him its annual alumni award. Like Jean Shepherd, a similarly mediocre student, Quin spent more time learning about life through ham radio. The radio waves opened up the world to him, cultures near and far, clodhoppers and elites alike. When he was feeling charitable, Quin even kibbitzed on the radio with White Sox fans.

Other times, he watched the nighttime shenanigans at the corner of Oak and Rush streets downtown, where his older brother had a third-floor apartment with a rooftop view. As Shepherd said, there are two kinds of education.

By shear grace, Quin got into the University of Illinois at Urbana-Champaign and earned three degrees, becoming "Dr. Q.," as his college students later dubbed him. And he started speaking and writing boat-loads of articles and books about culture, religion, and communication—three essential subjects that capture human experience.

Listening to radio raconteur Shepherd late at night, Dr. Q studied how the avuncular "Shep" told tales so engagingly. Eventually, Professor Schultze invited Jean to teach storytelling with him. Dr. Q and Shep exchanged tales and techniques, truths and exaggerations, about the everyday aspects of life that most North Americans take for granted. In Dr. Q's estimation, Jean was one of the greatest American storytellers of the 20th century. The grateful professor remains honored to have learned from a master.

Contact Dr. Q at qschultze@gmail.com. Or try calling K8QS on 17 meters in the afternoon, when the sunspots are hopping; you might even hear the ghost of Jean emanating from the ether hanging over Lake Michigan and infusing the fetid ponds by the steel mills near Hammond.

P.S.—Some of Dr. Q's speeches and ruminations are available at:
**www.quentinschultze.com**

His Shepherdesque videos about this book are posted at
**https://www.youtube.com/@YoullShootYourEyeOutBook**

You can purchase personally signed copies of this book at
**https://quentin-schultze.square.site/**

Excelsior!

Made in United States
Troutdale, OR
12/20/2024

27012667R00117